THIS BOOK BELONGS TO

Cape Turnaround™ Collective
Blank Manuscript Paper (6x9)
120 Total Pages

Send Questions & Inquiries to
info@capeturnaround.com

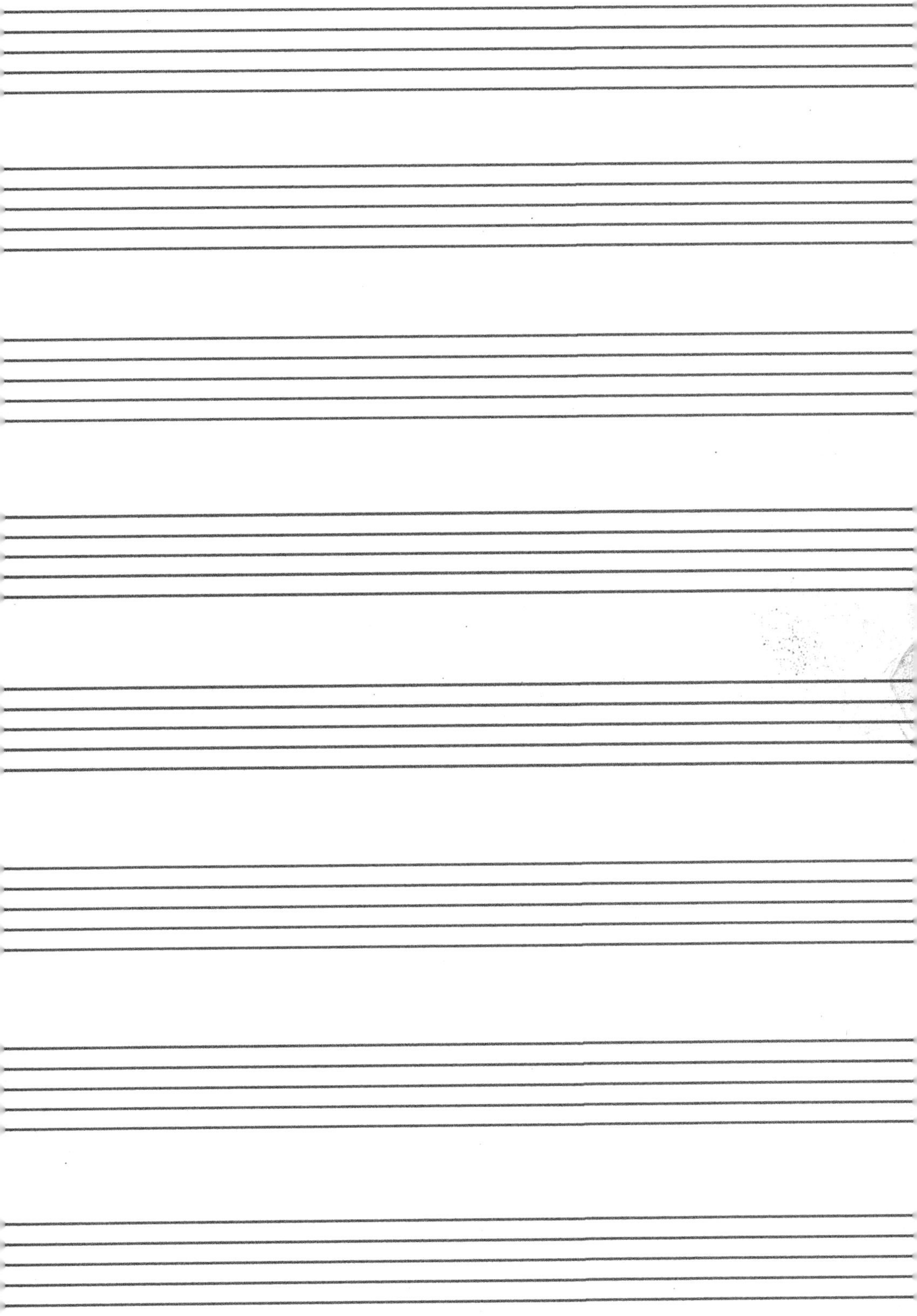

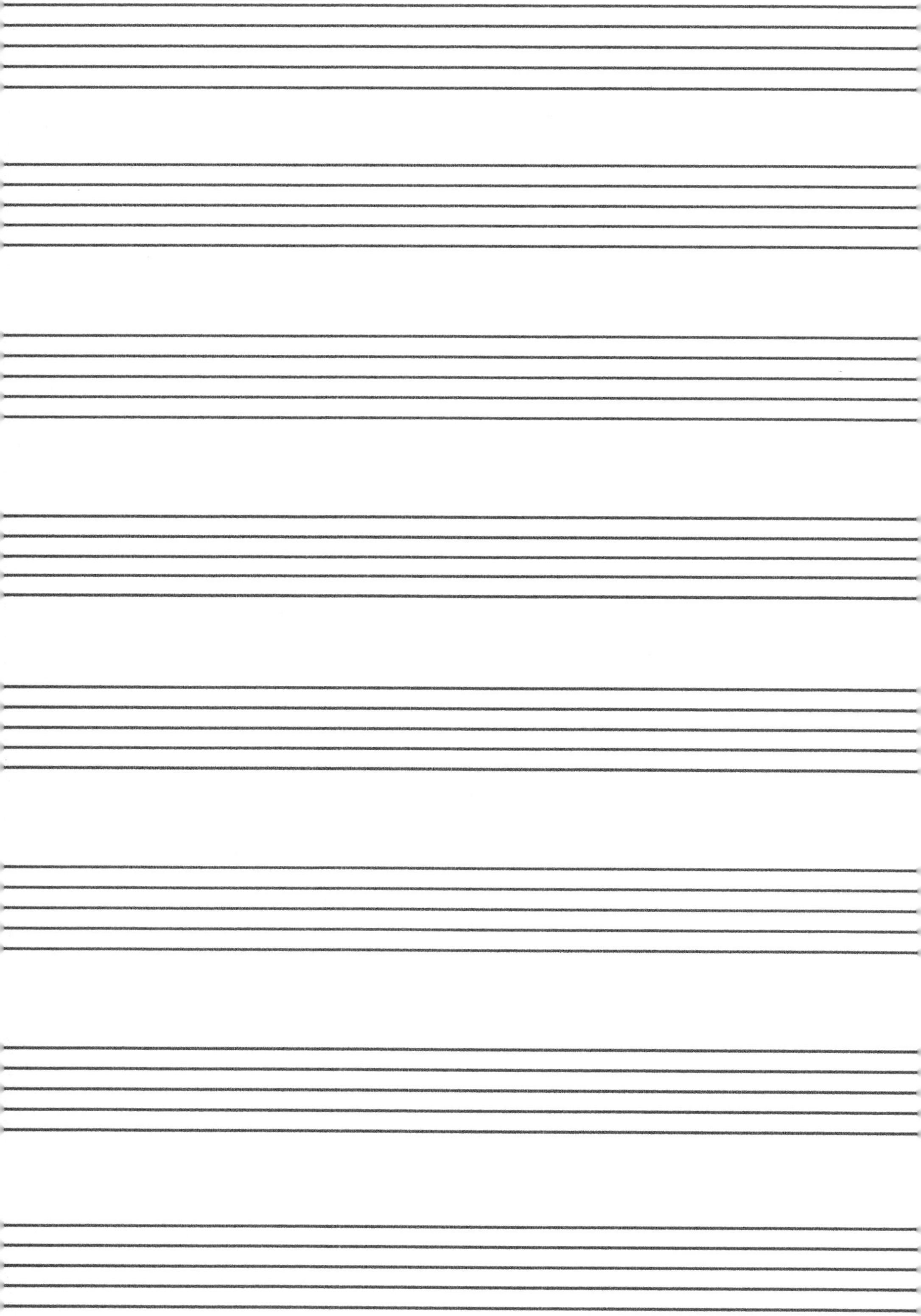

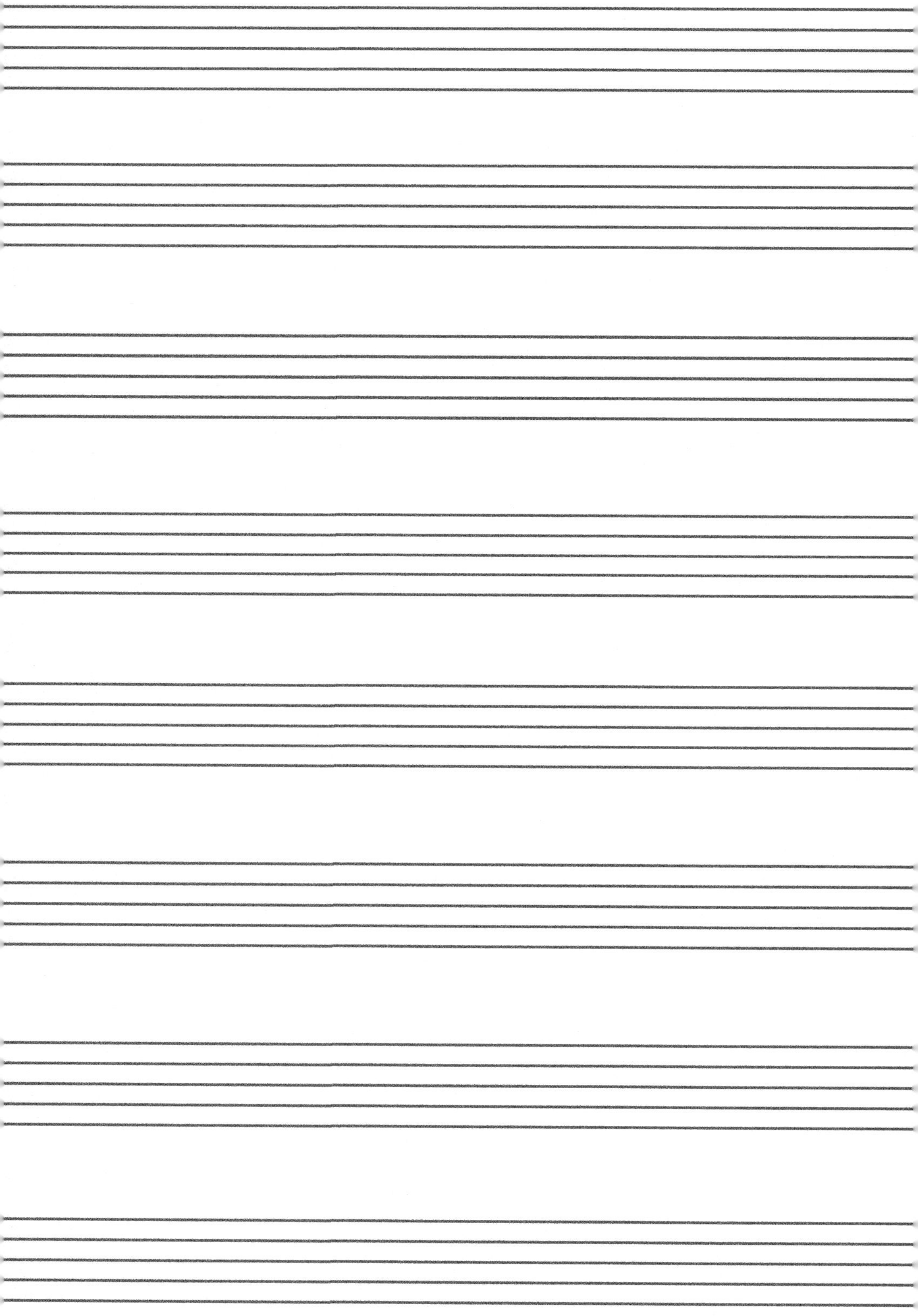

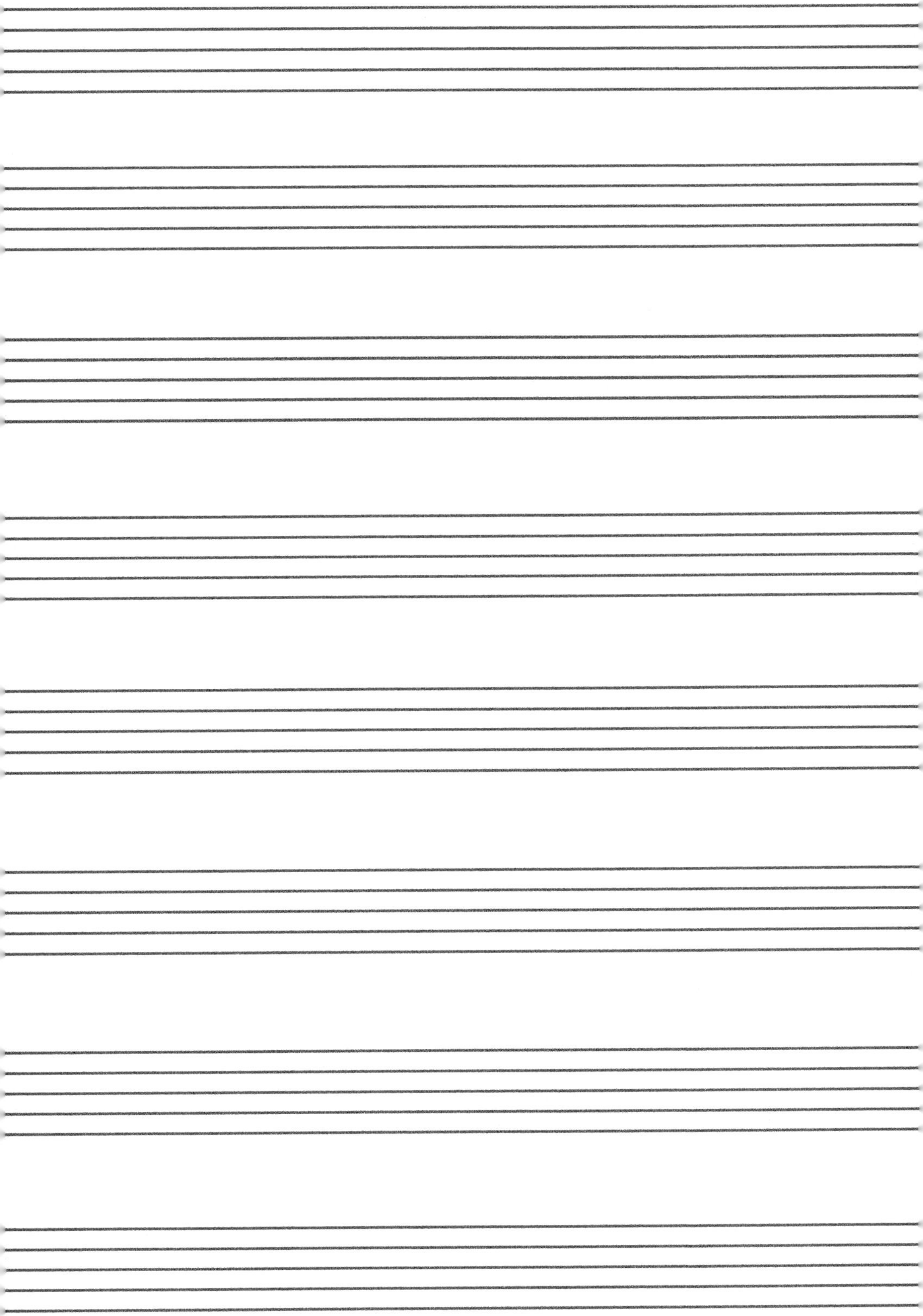

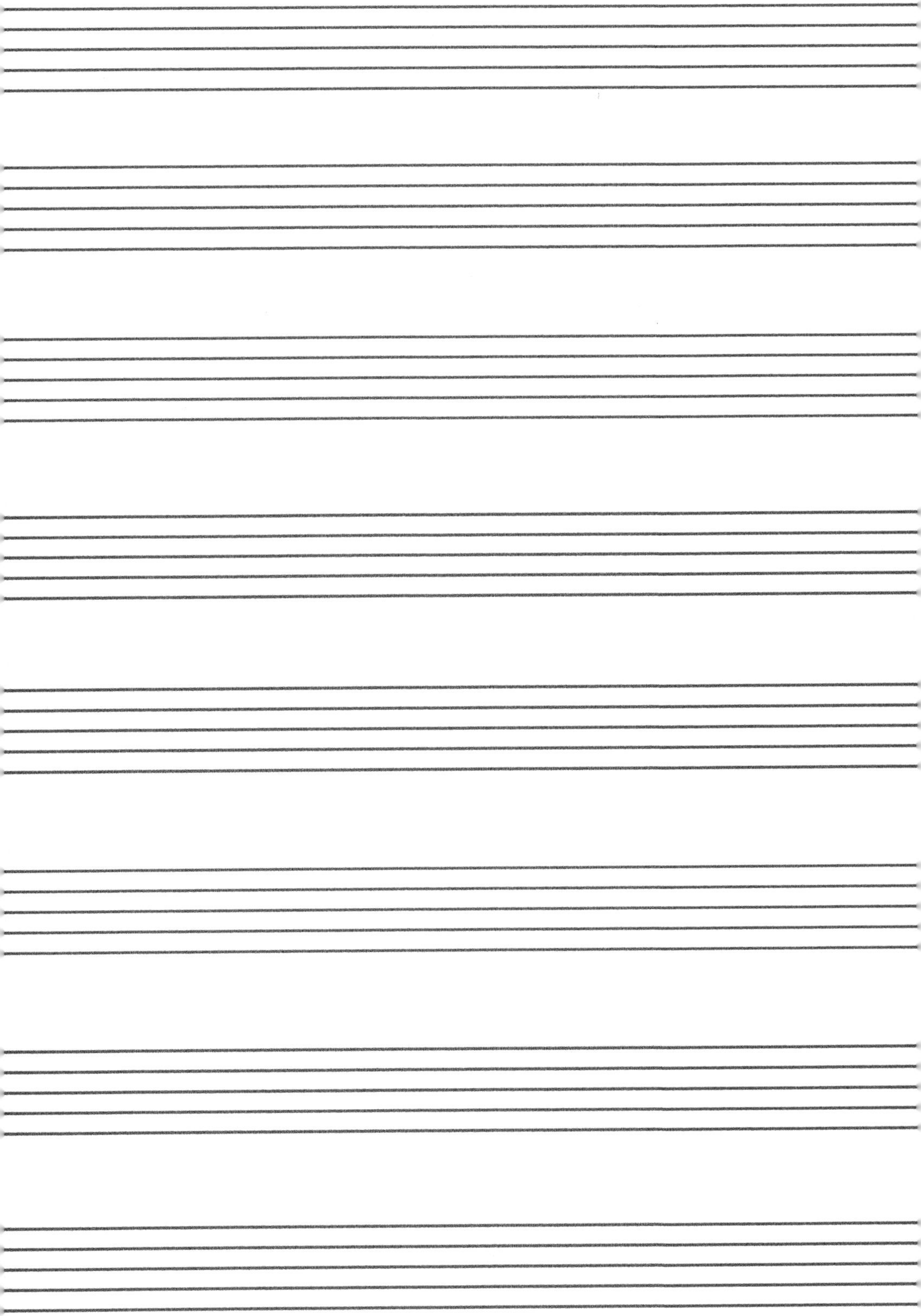

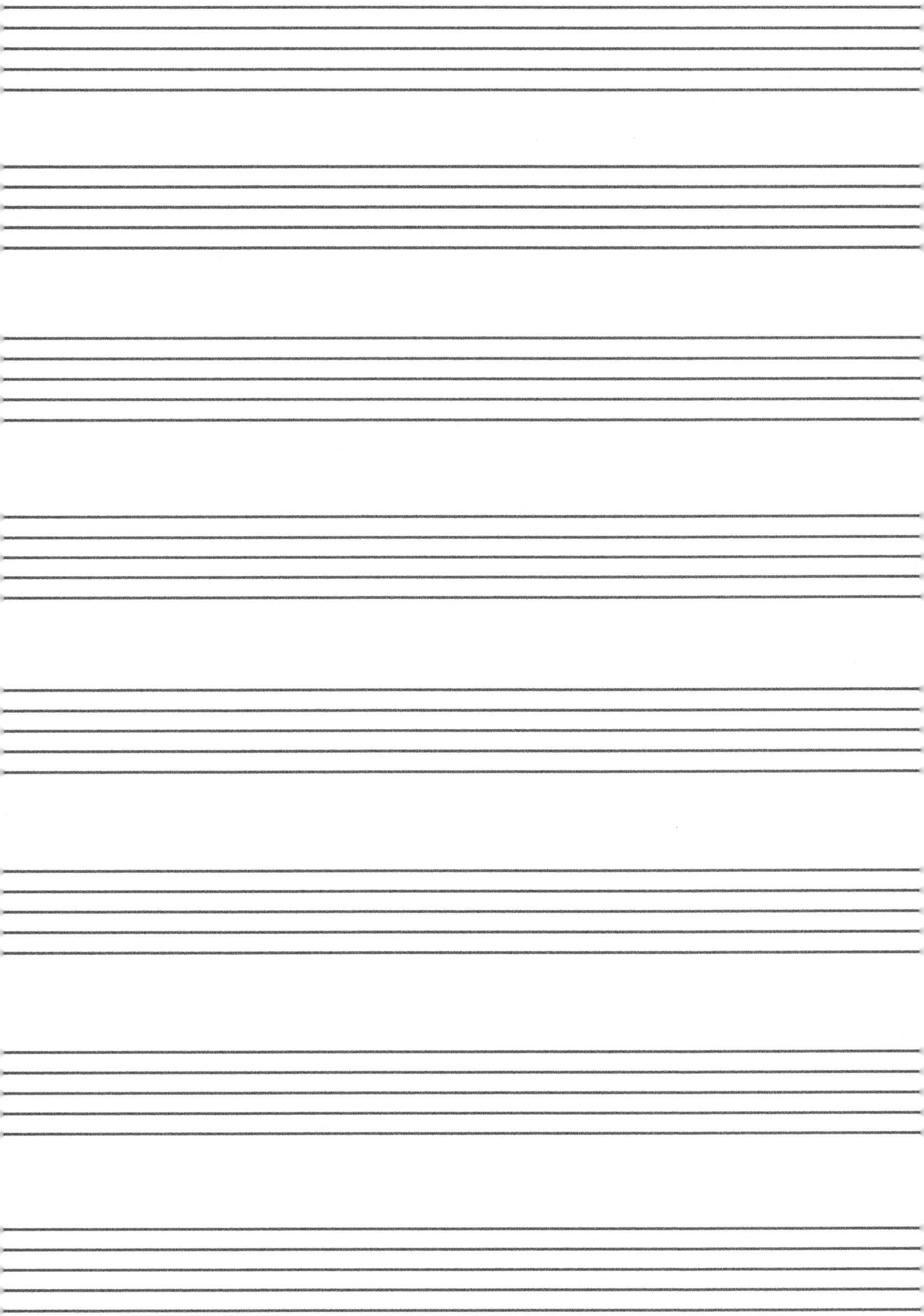

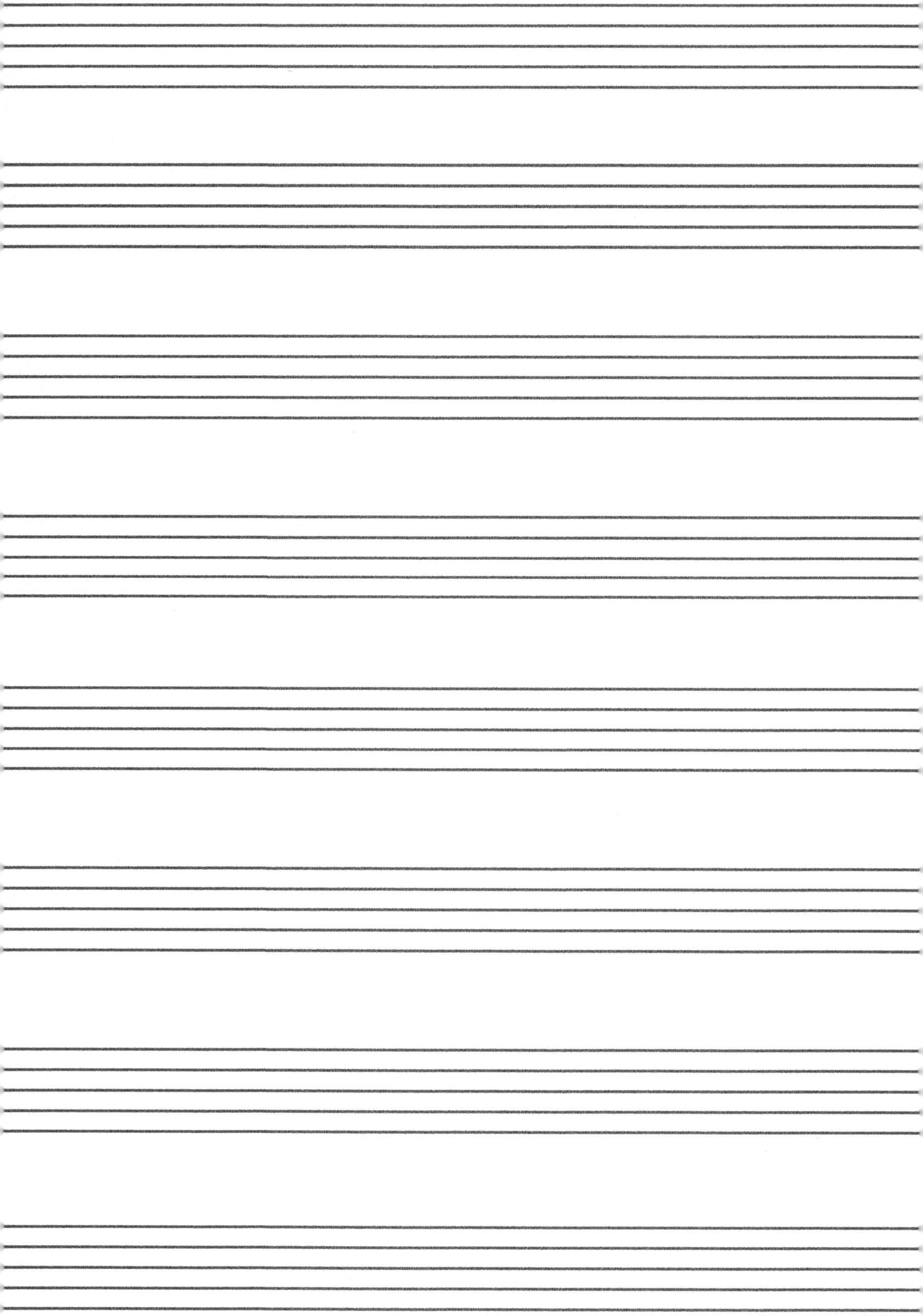

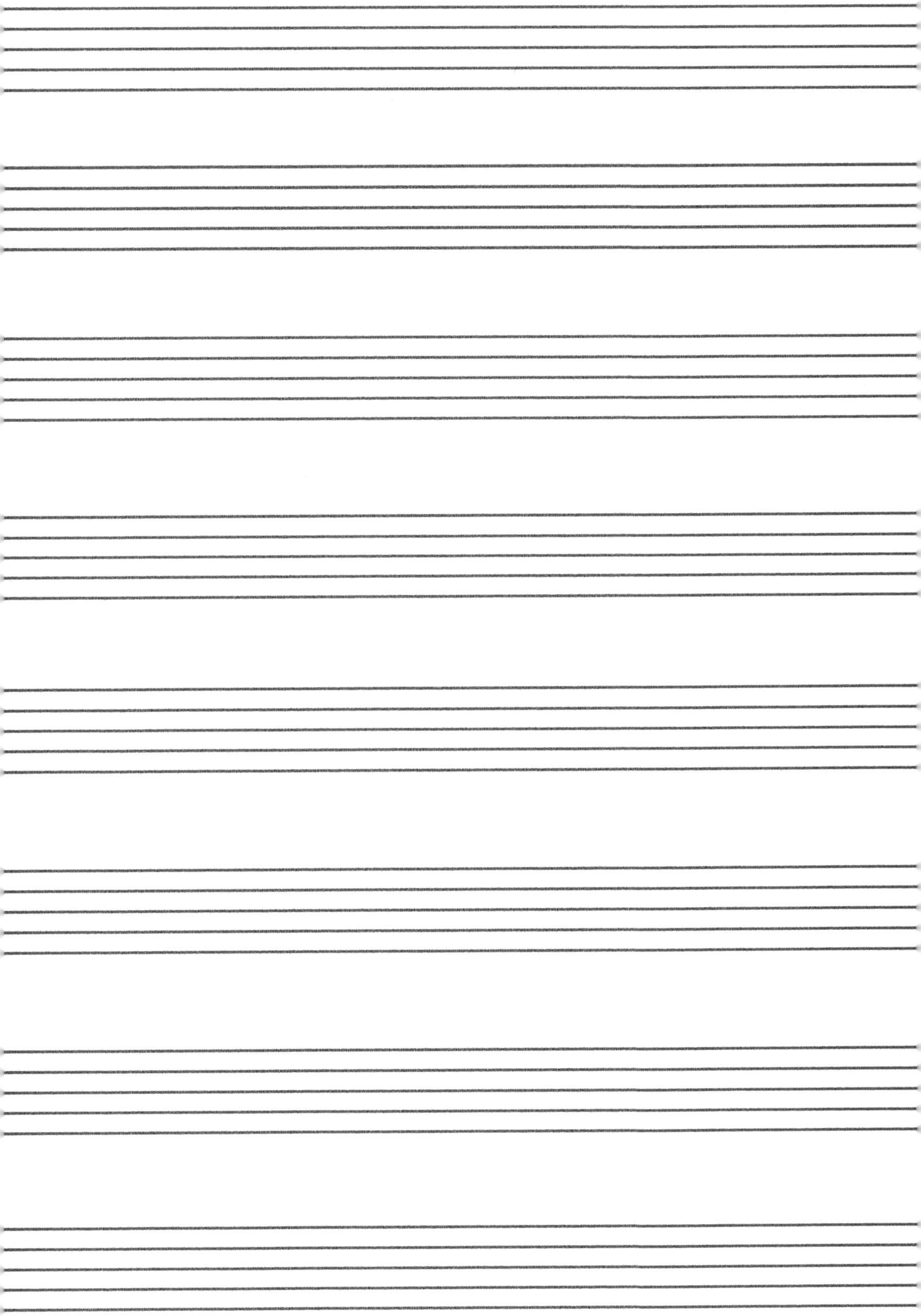

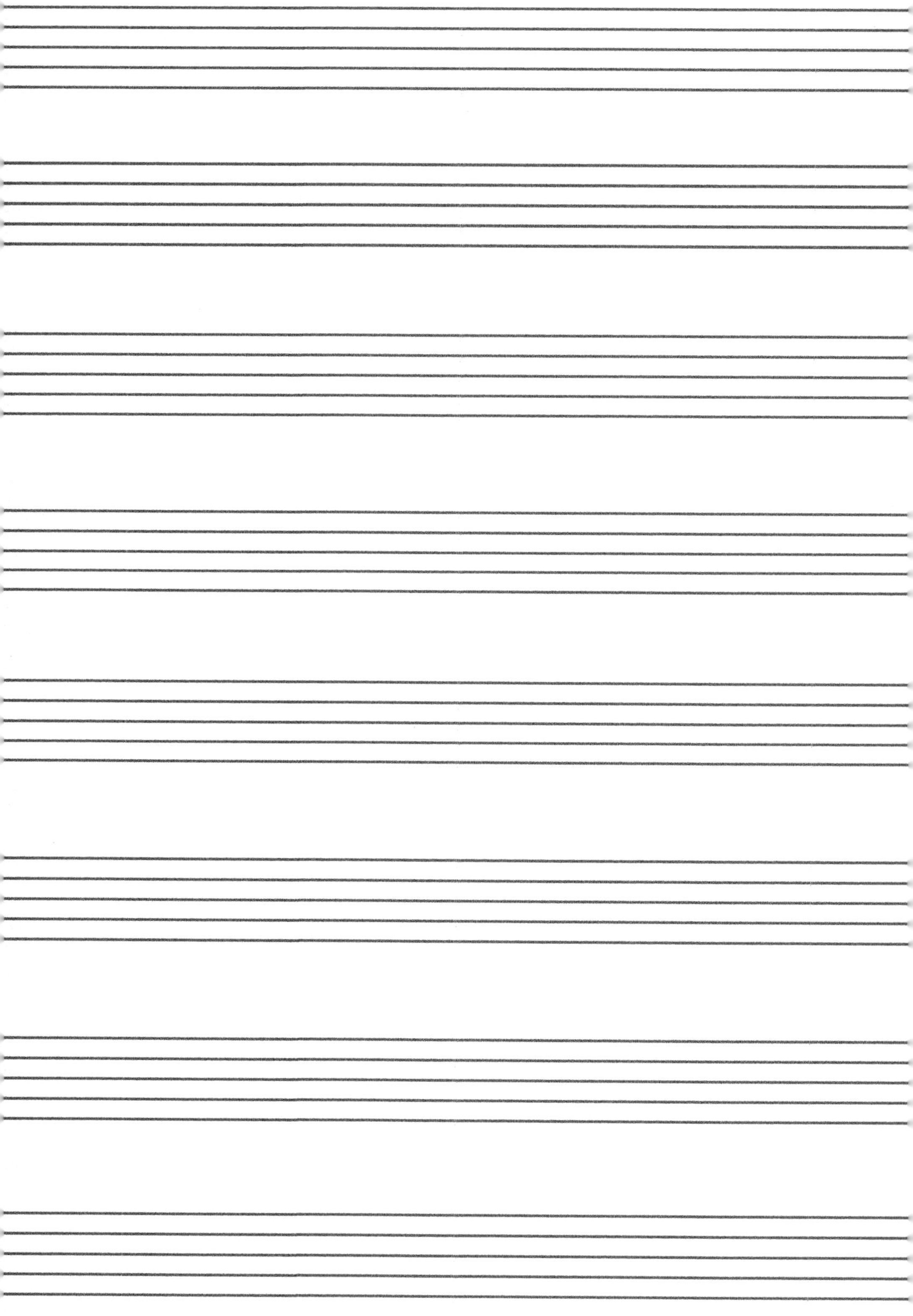

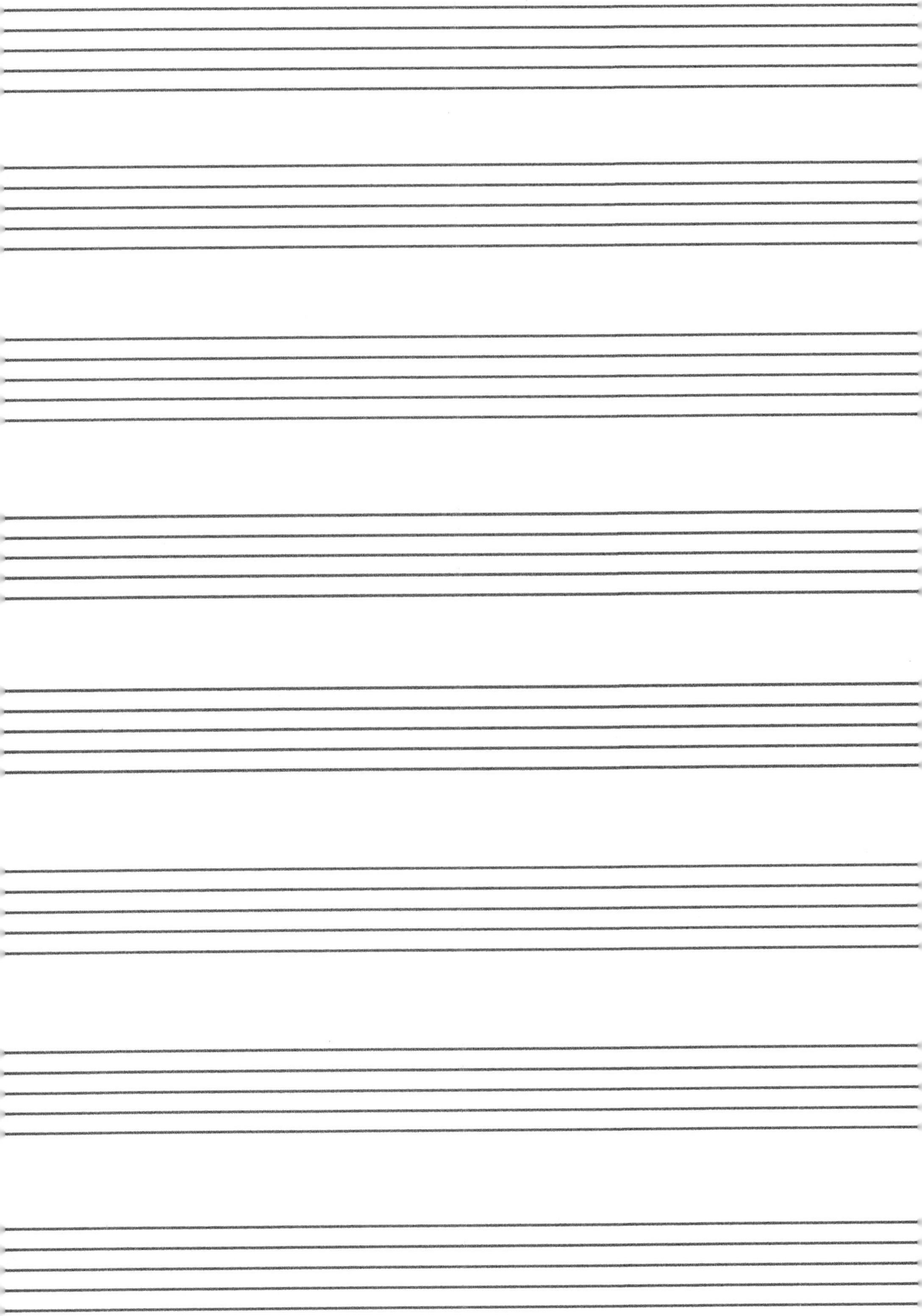

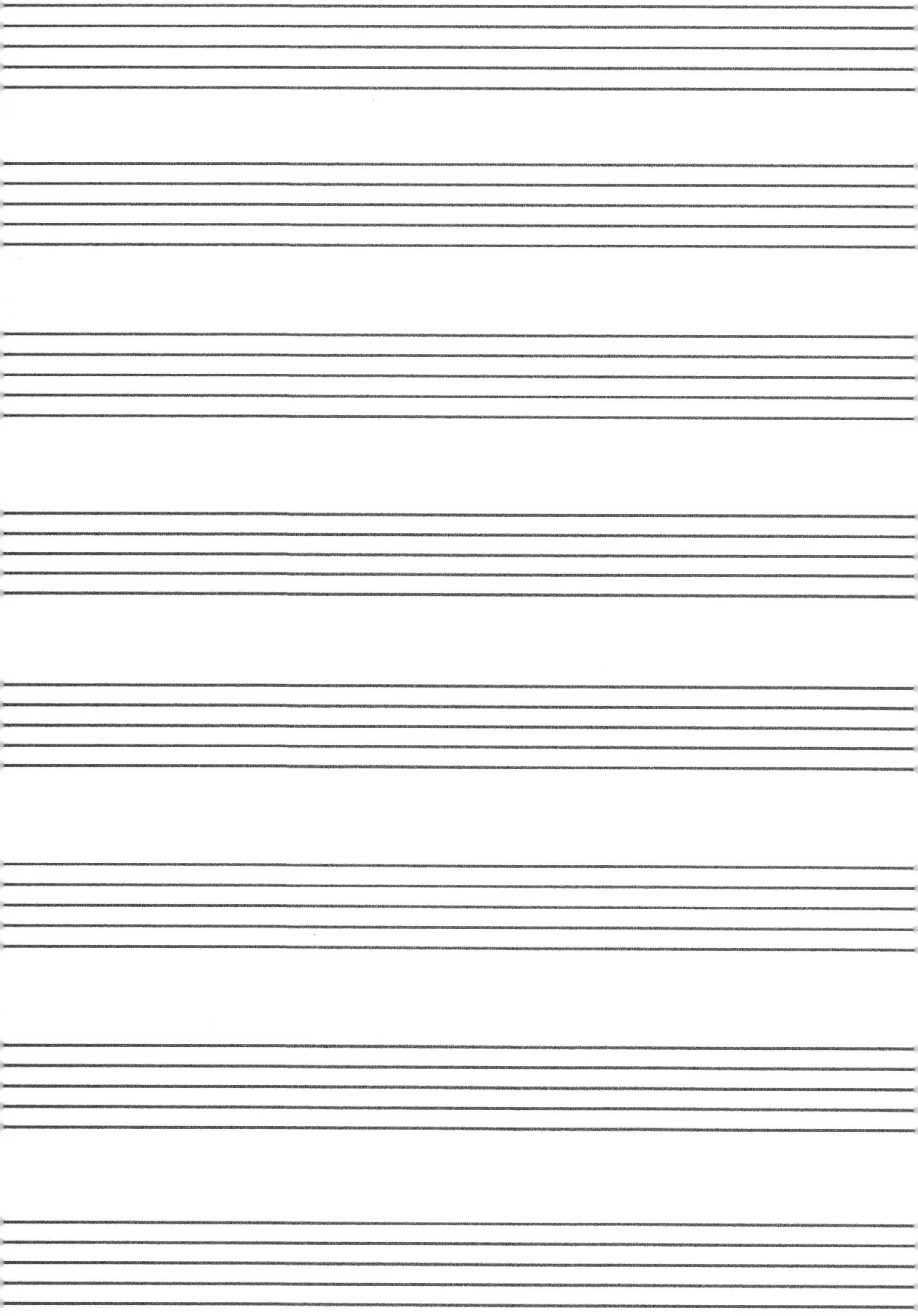

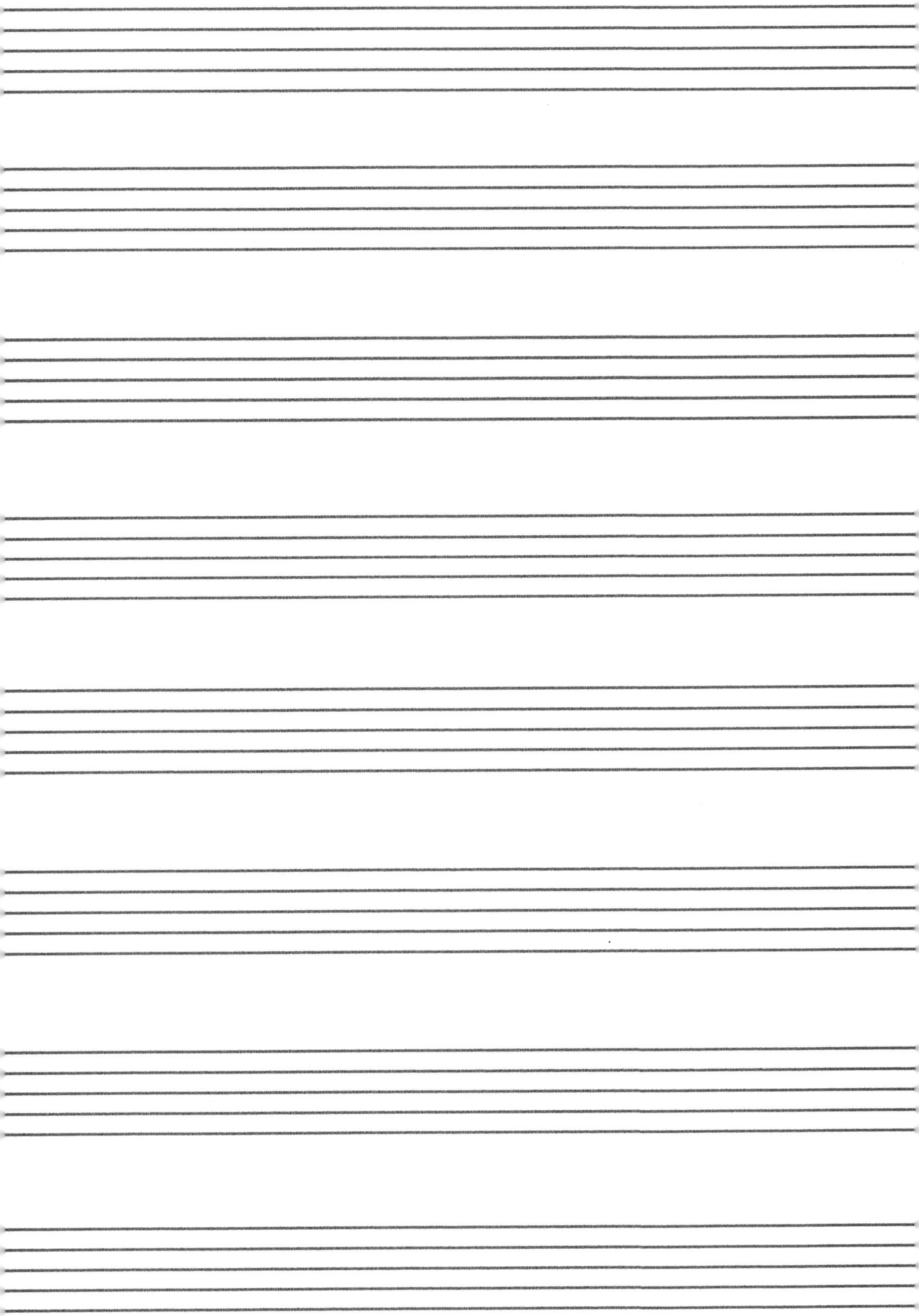

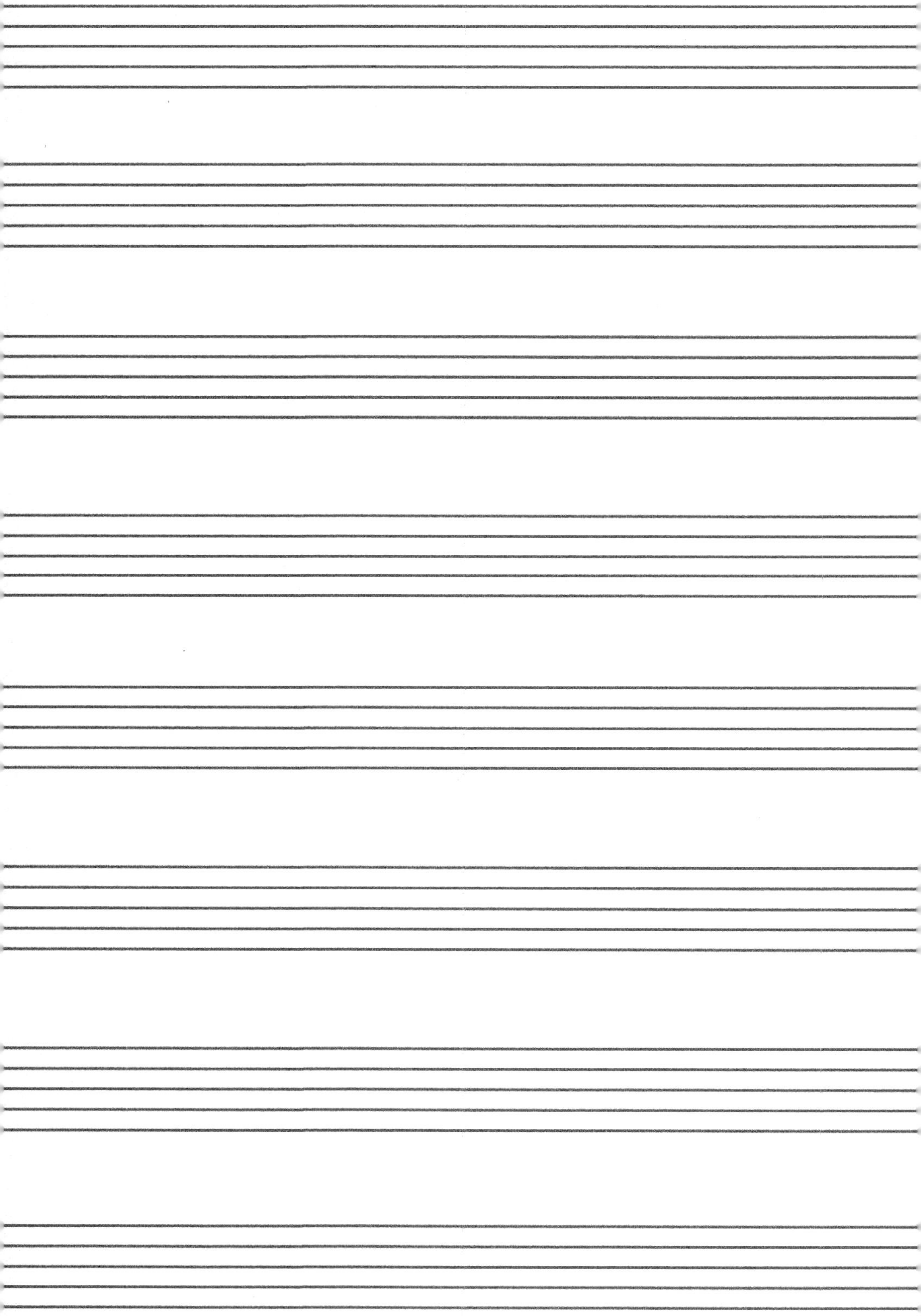

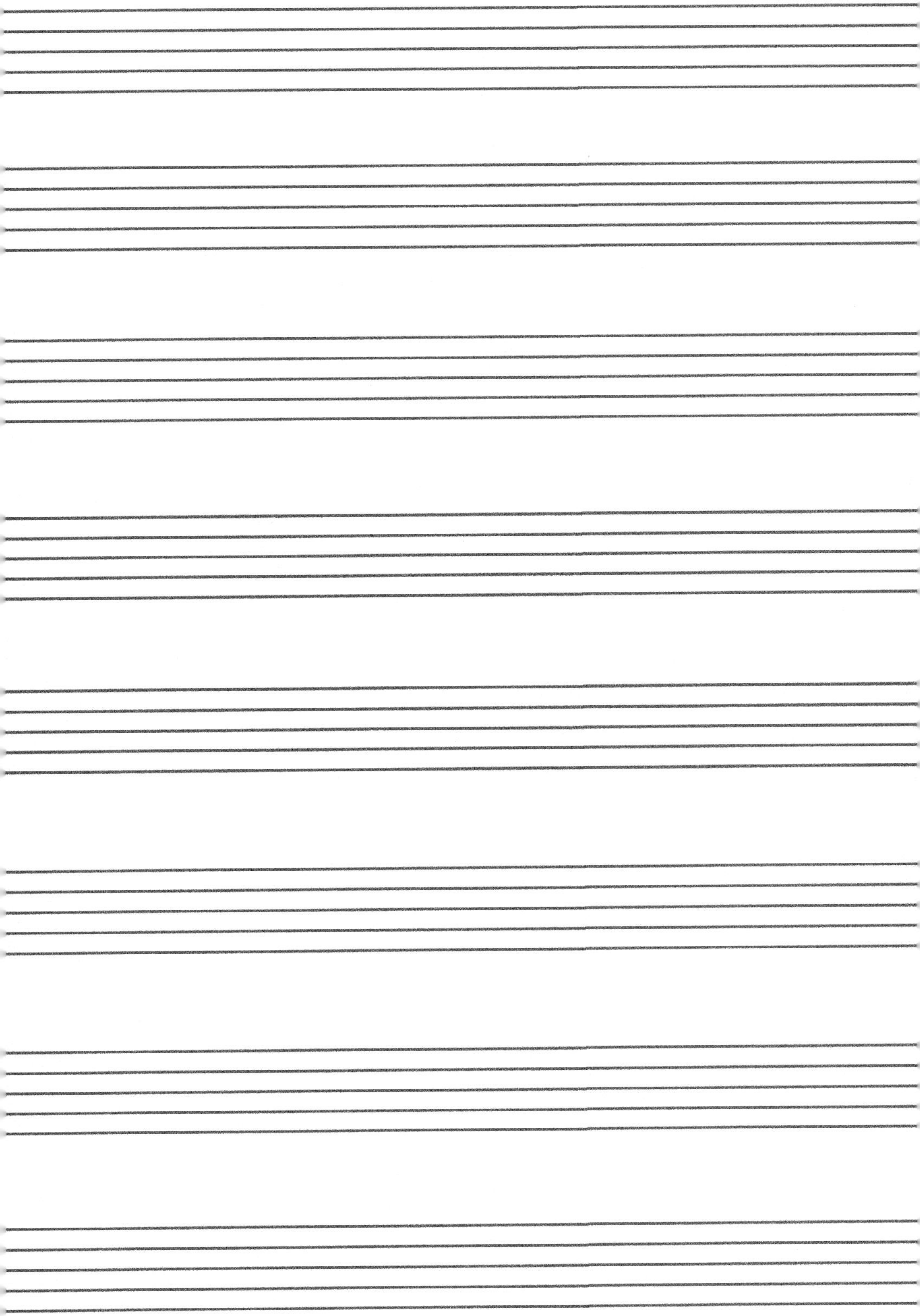

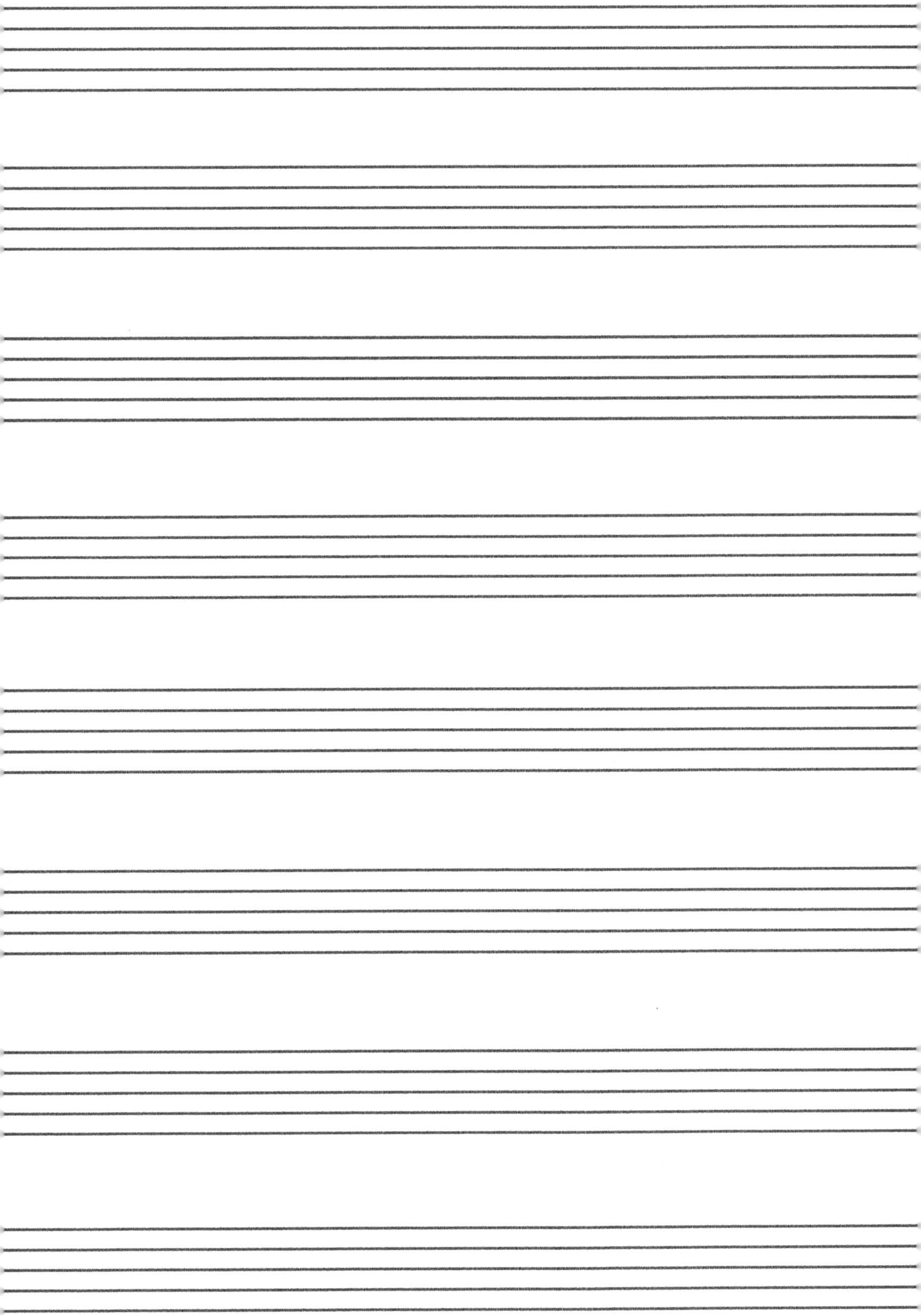

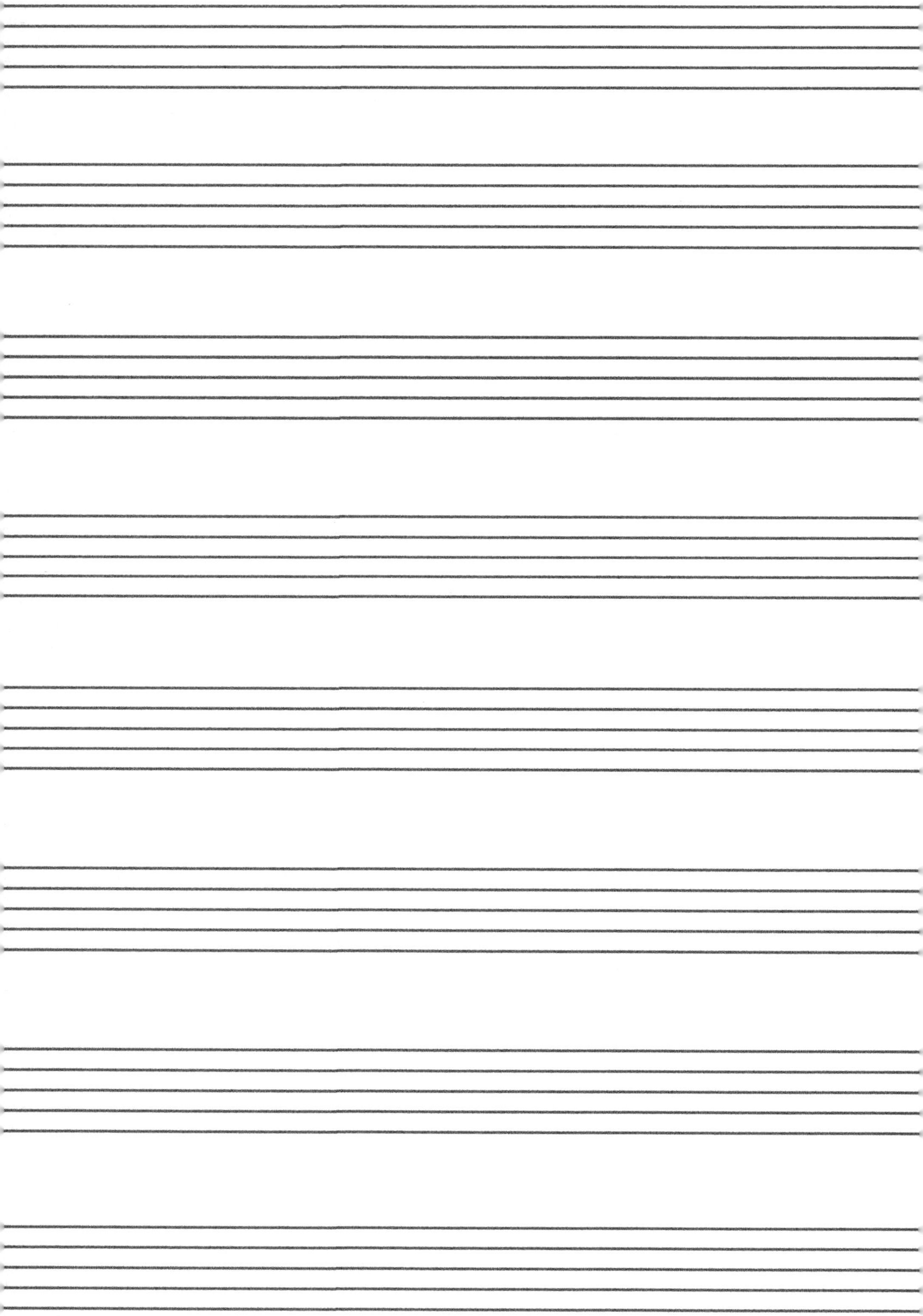

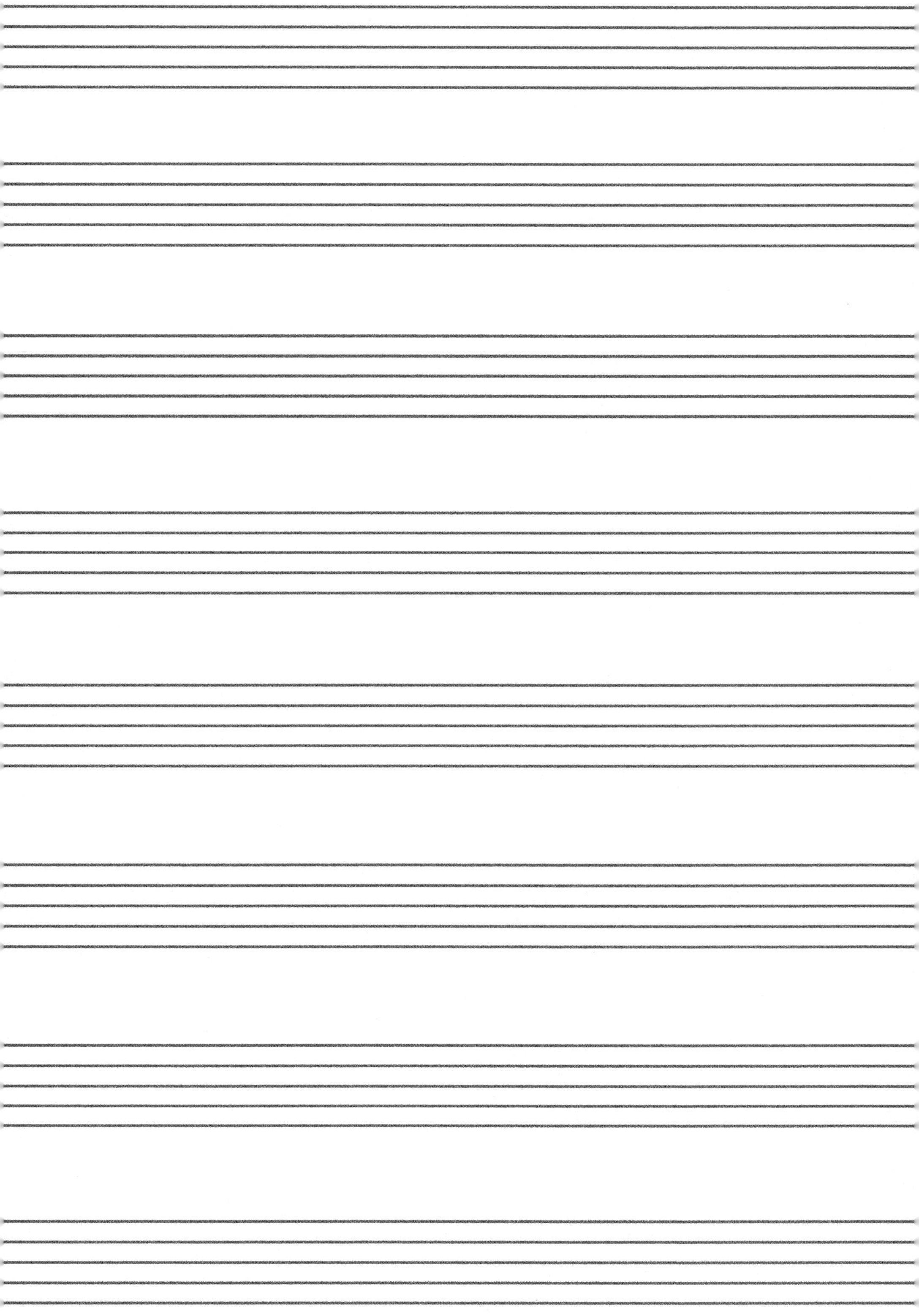

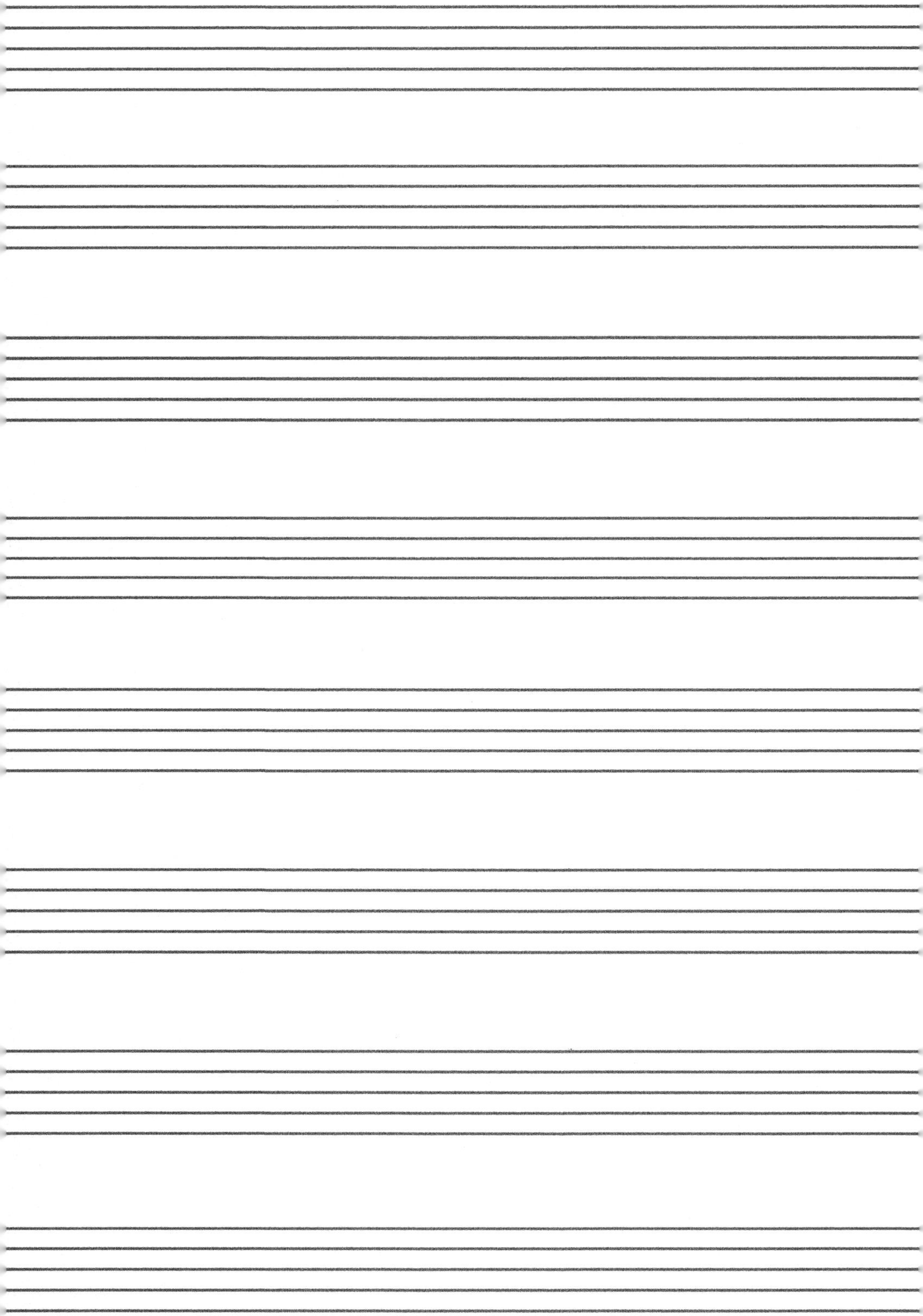

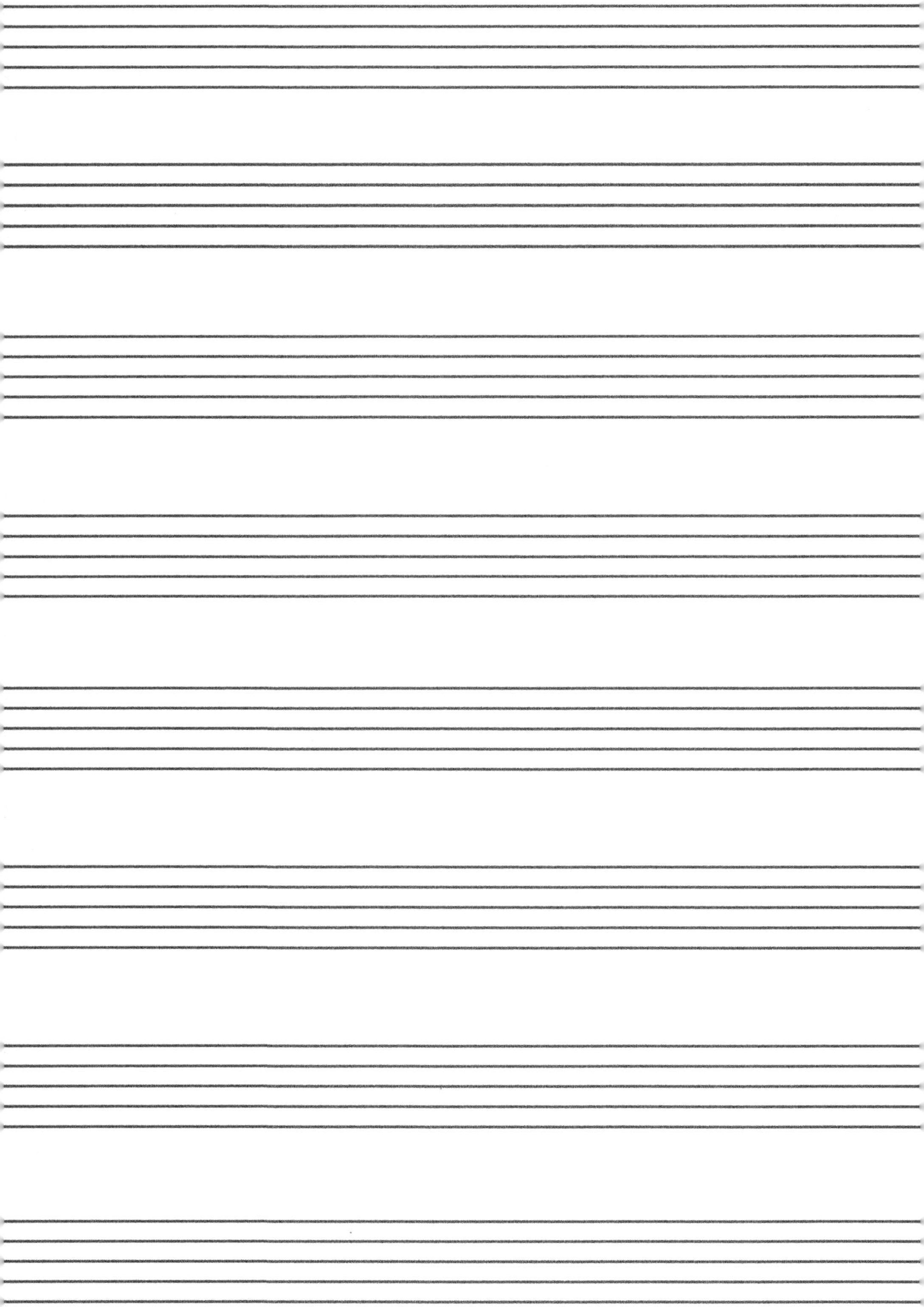

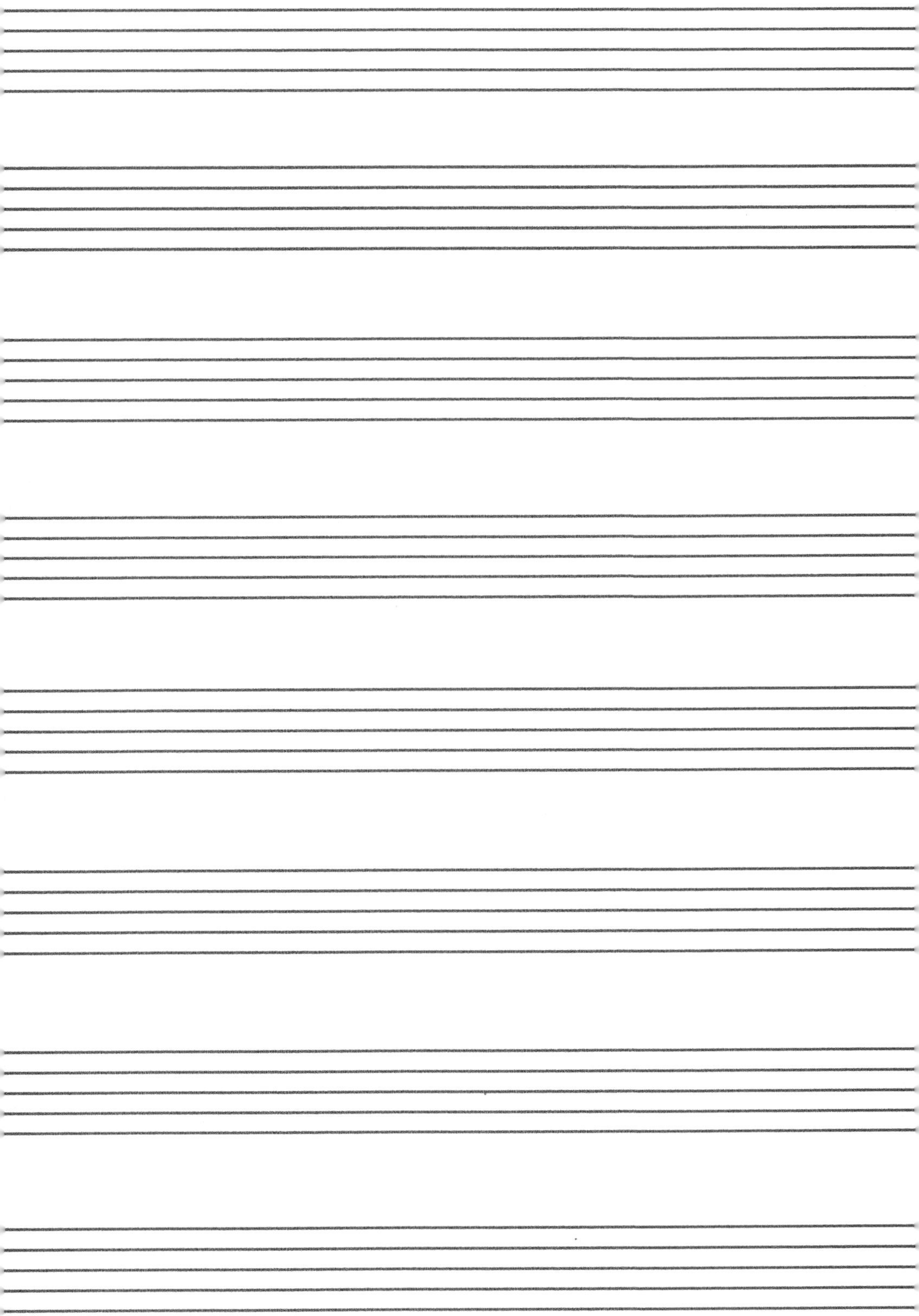

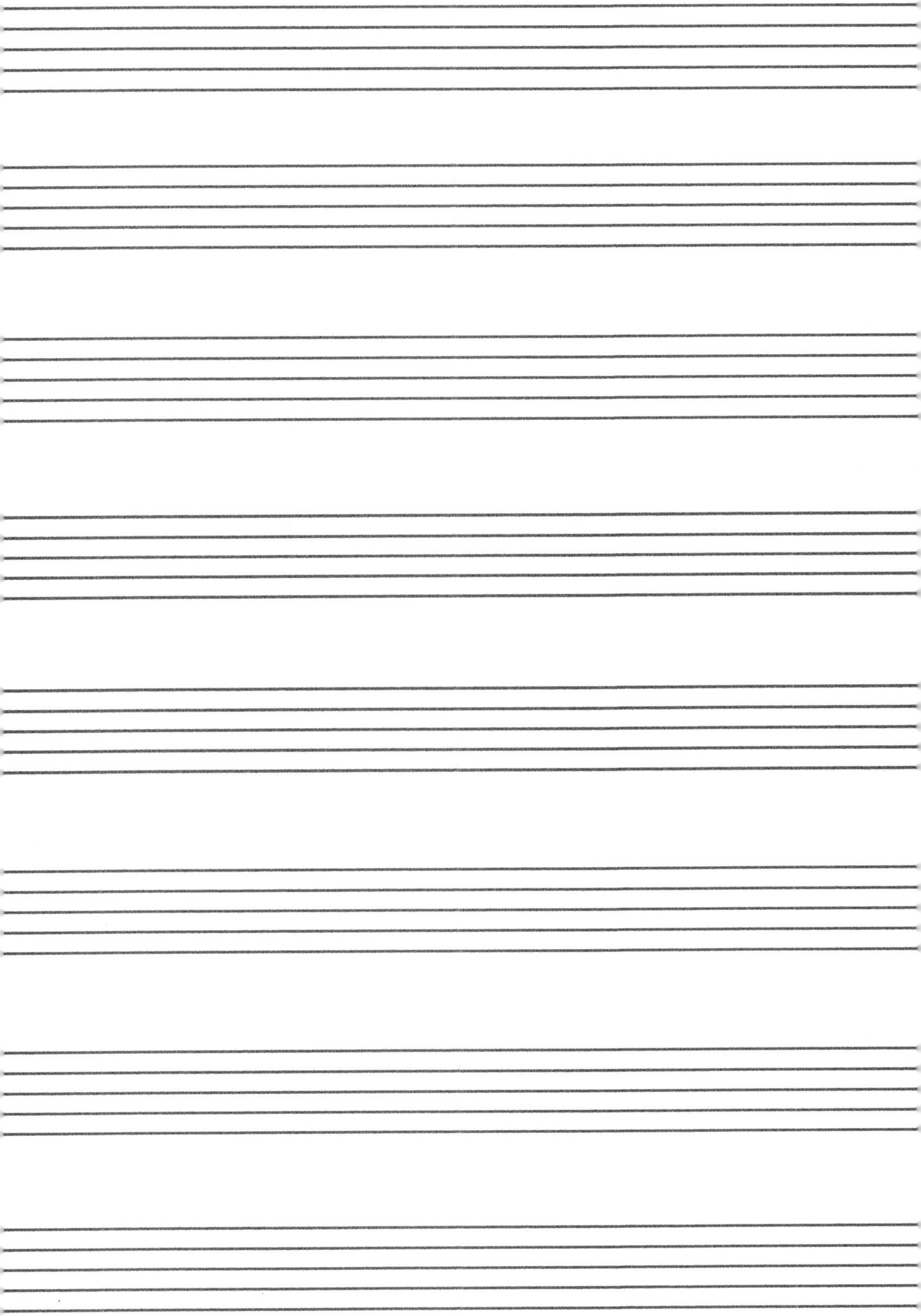

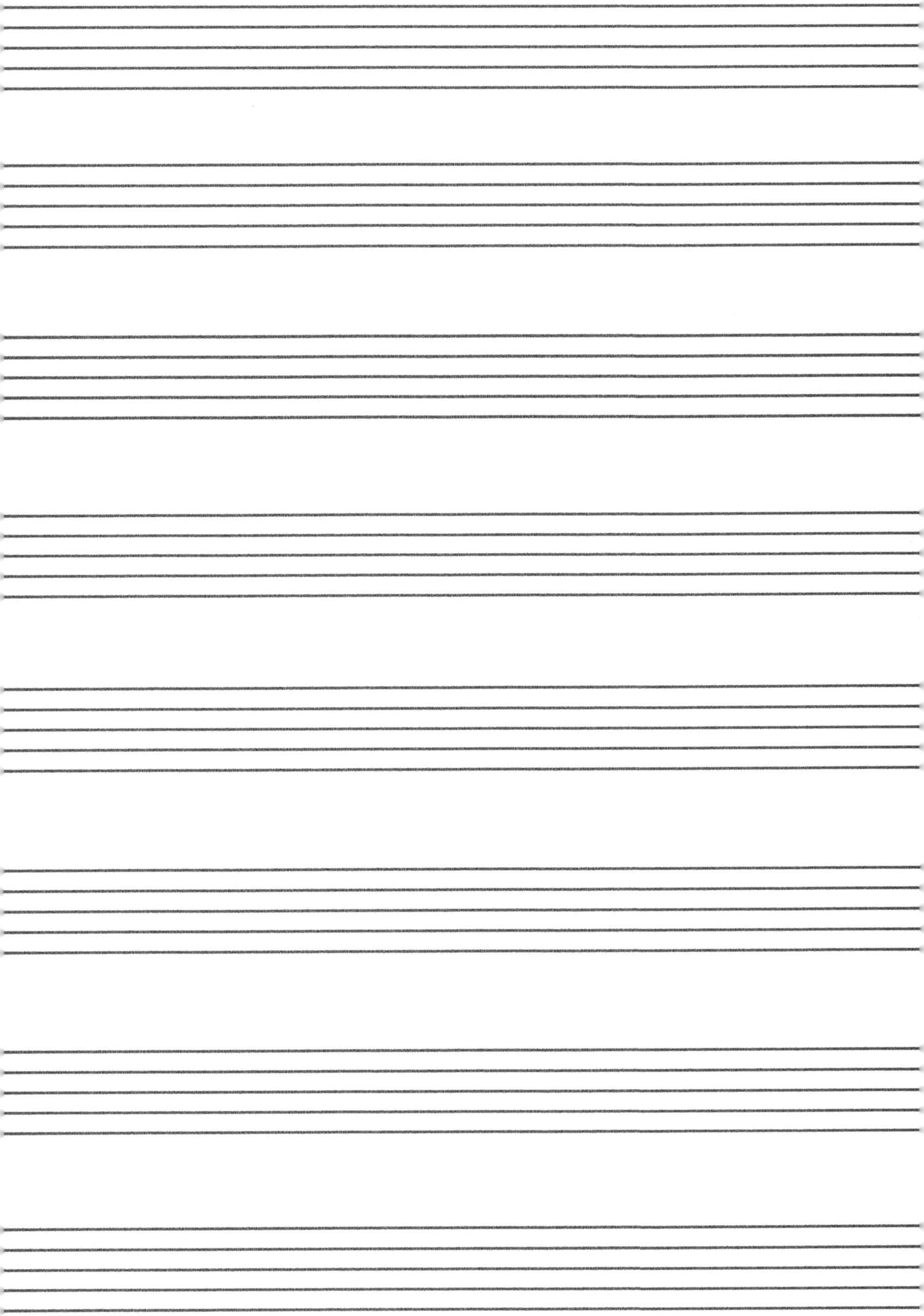

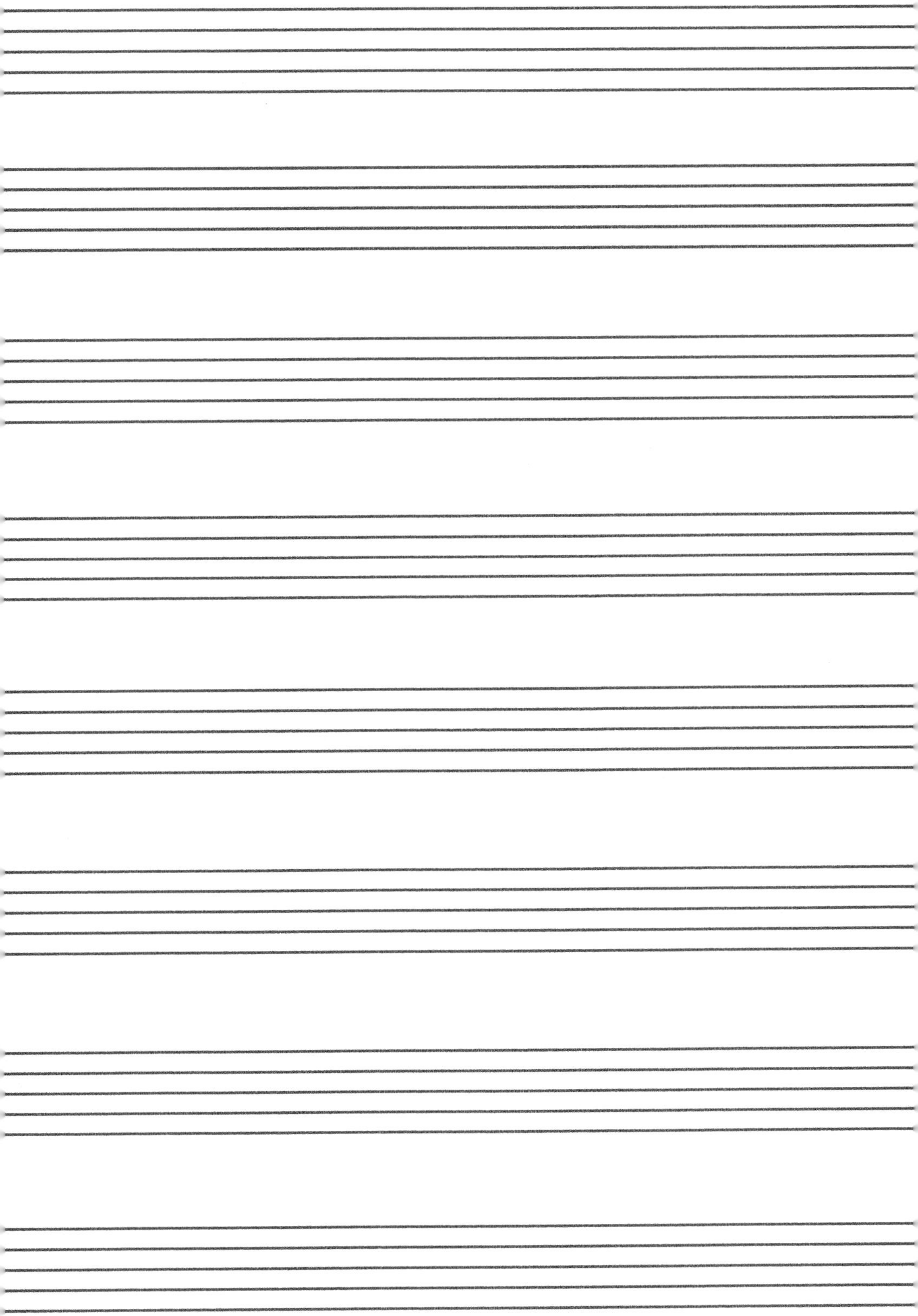

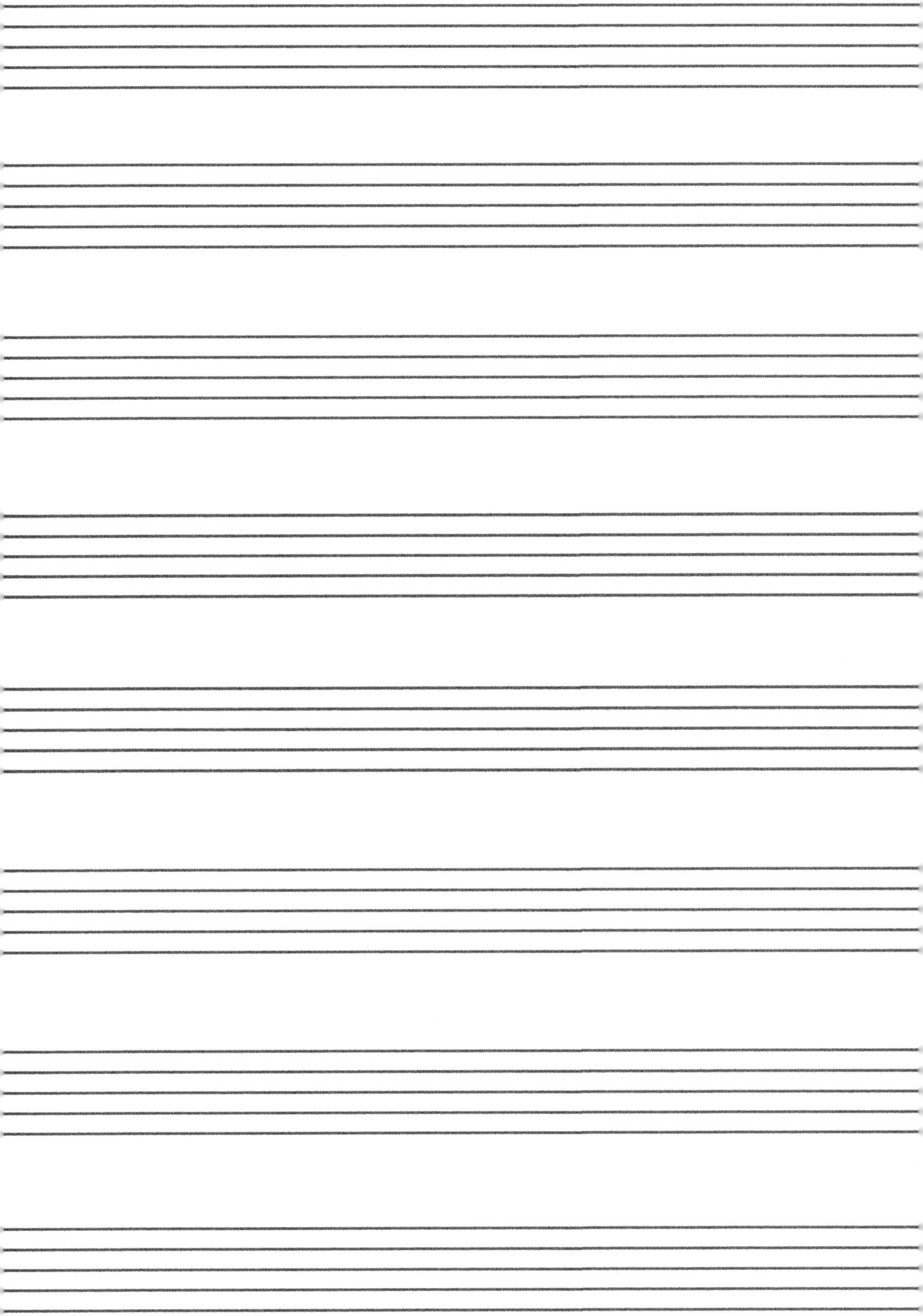

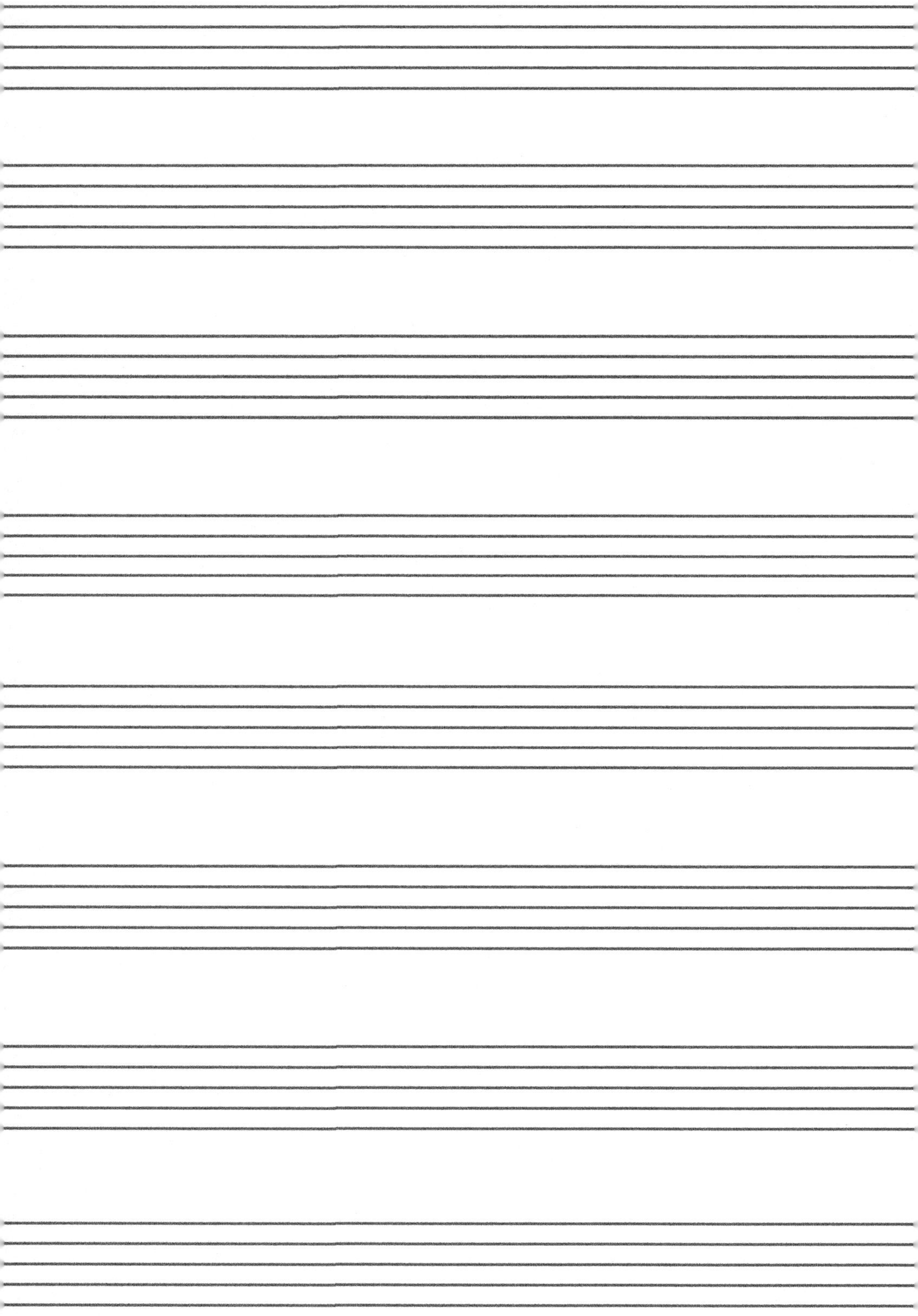

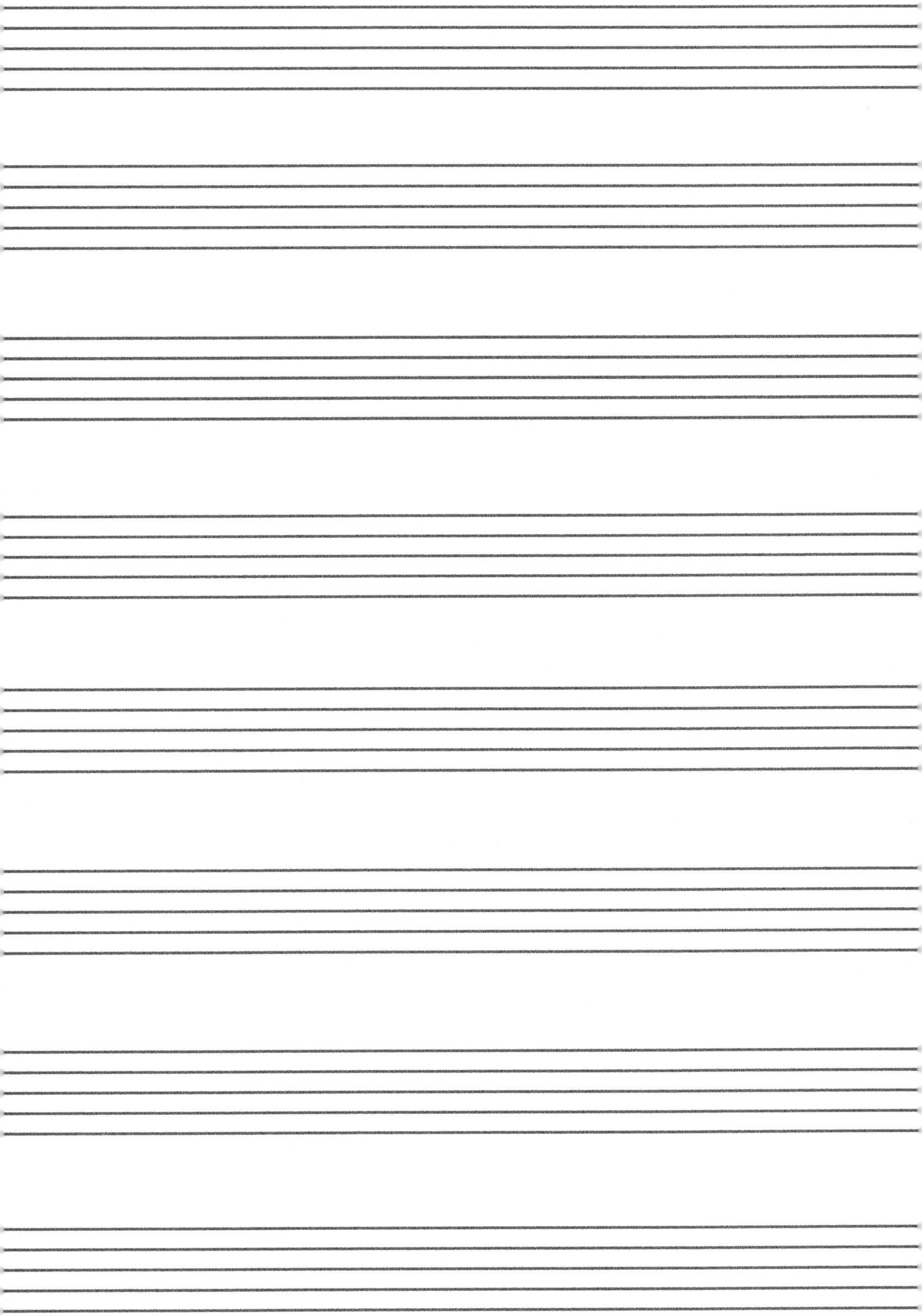

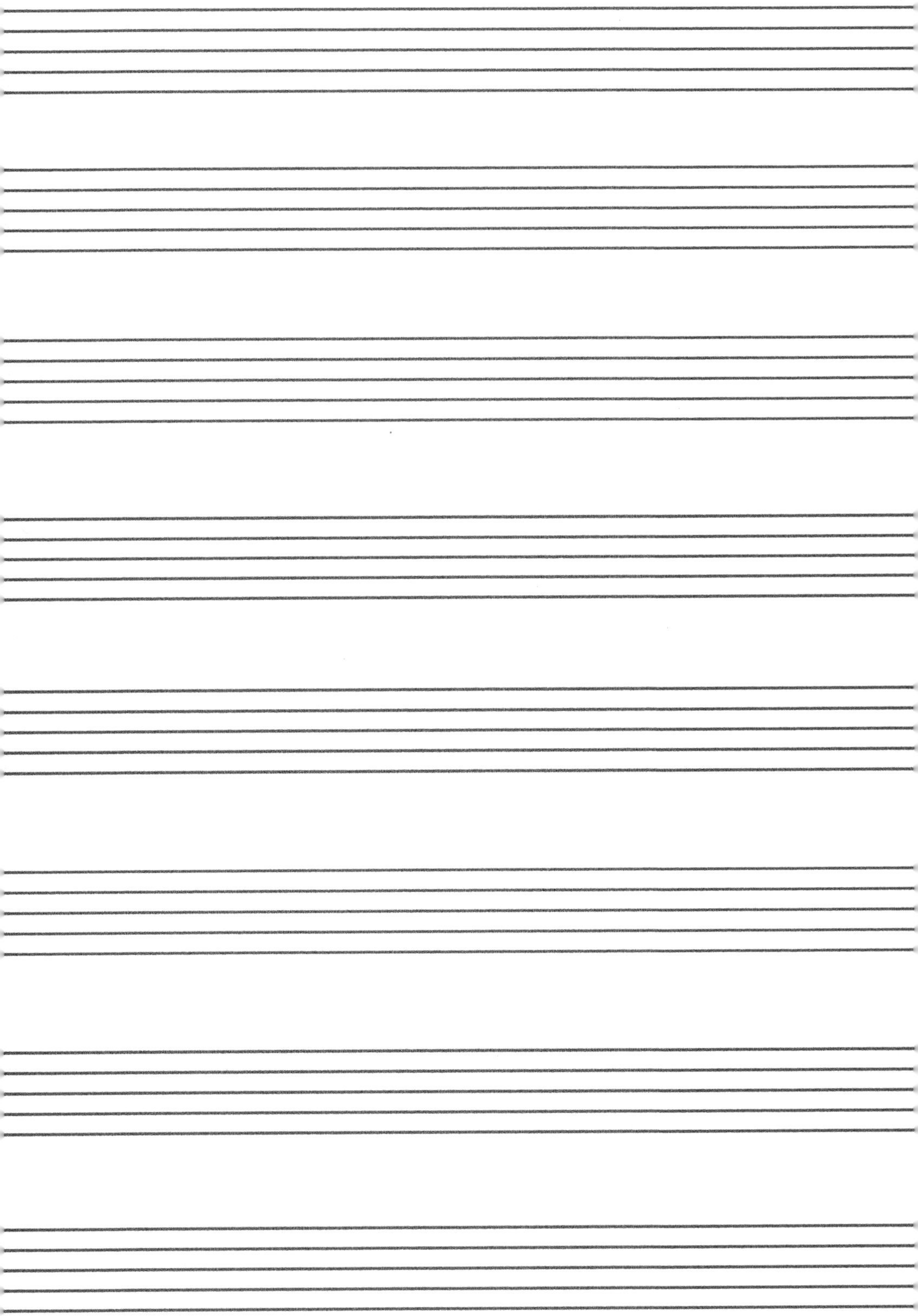

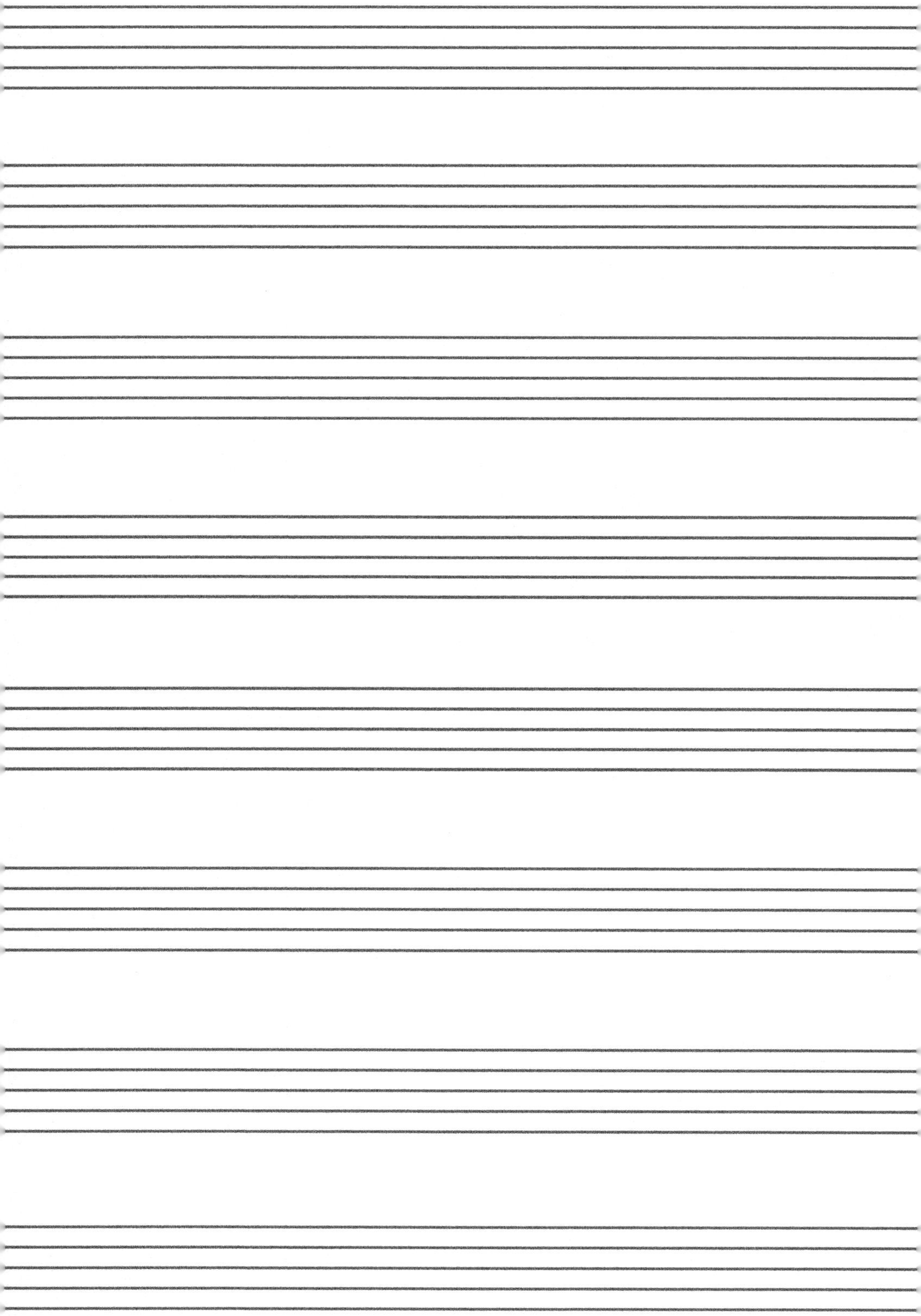

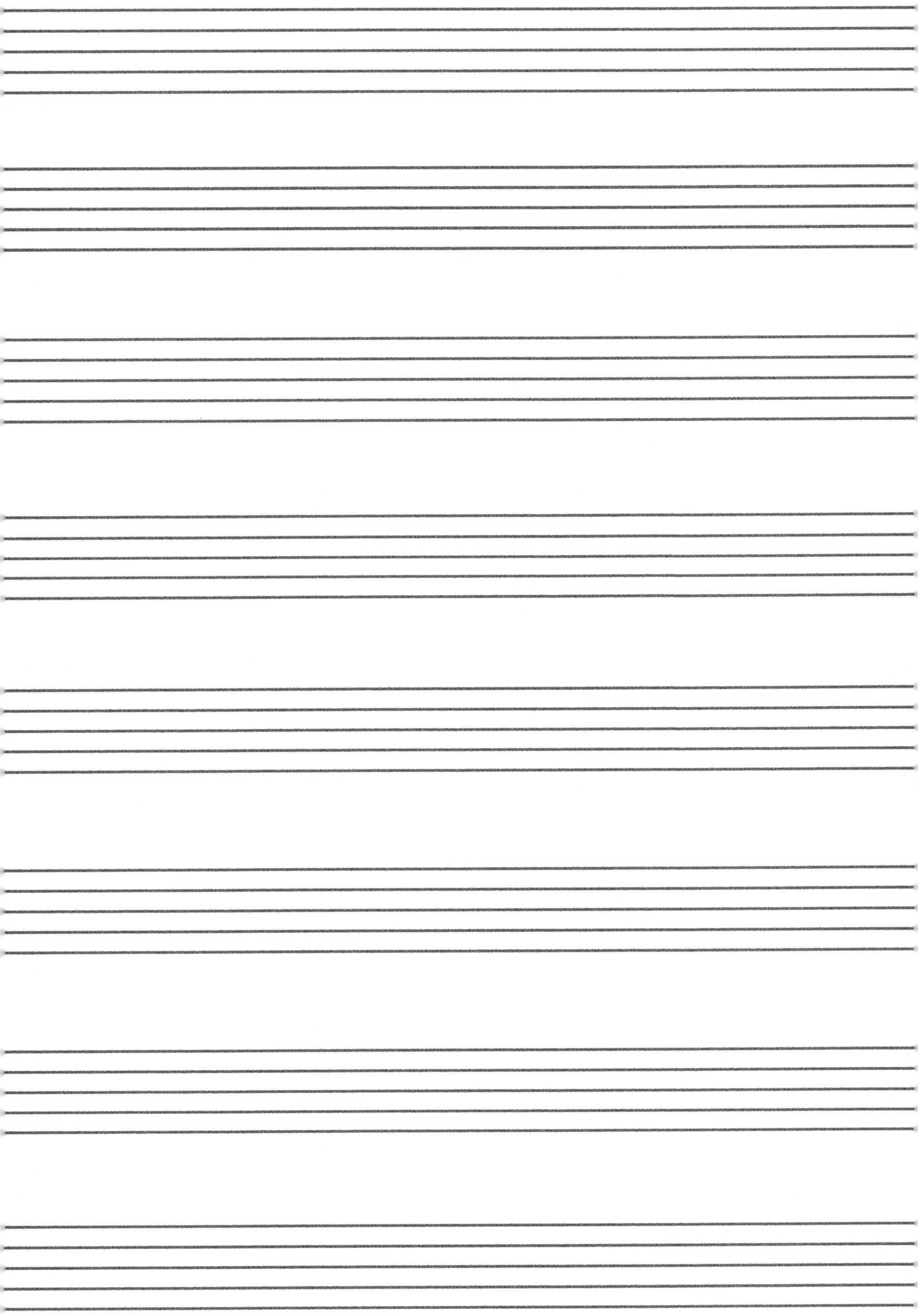

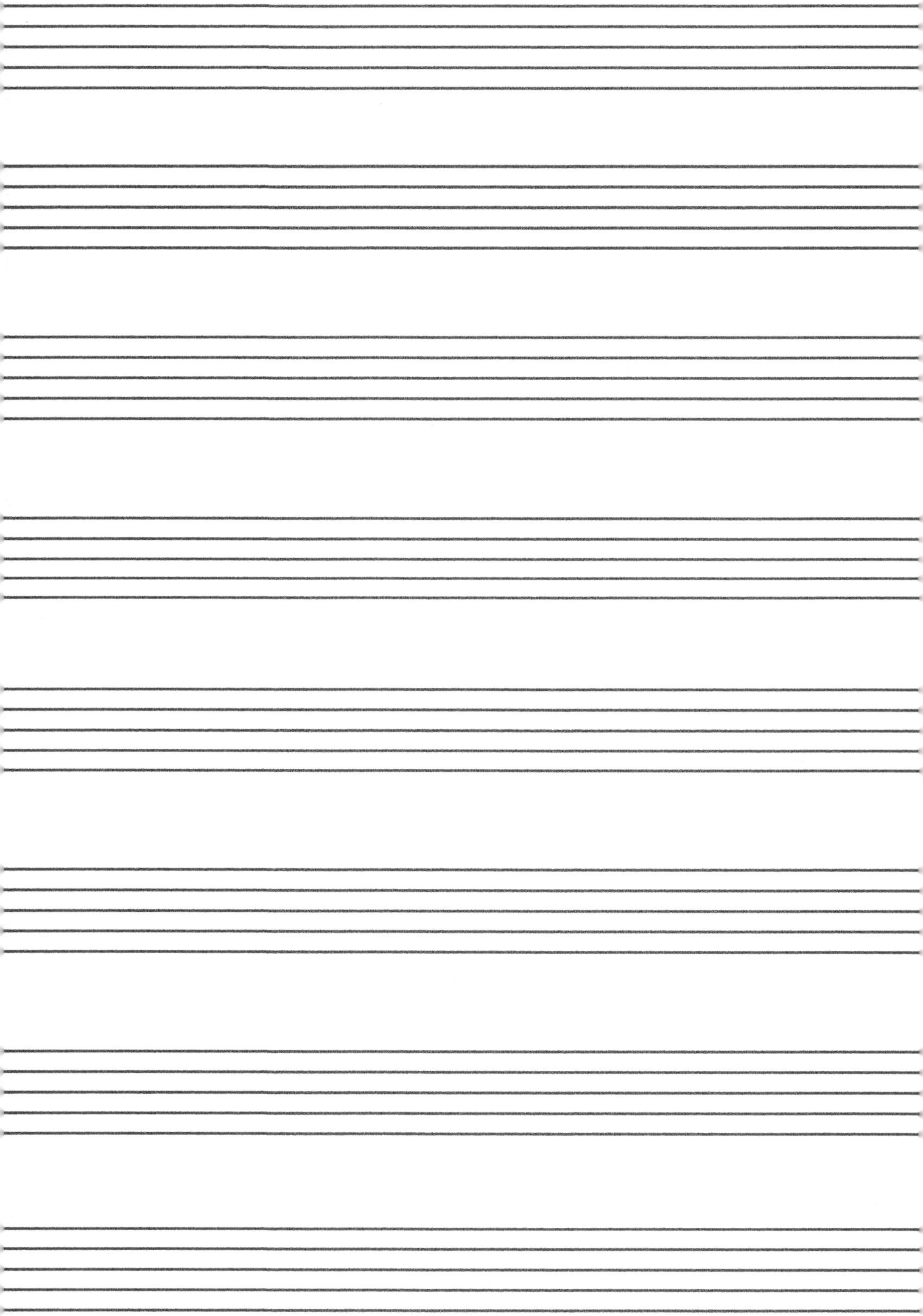

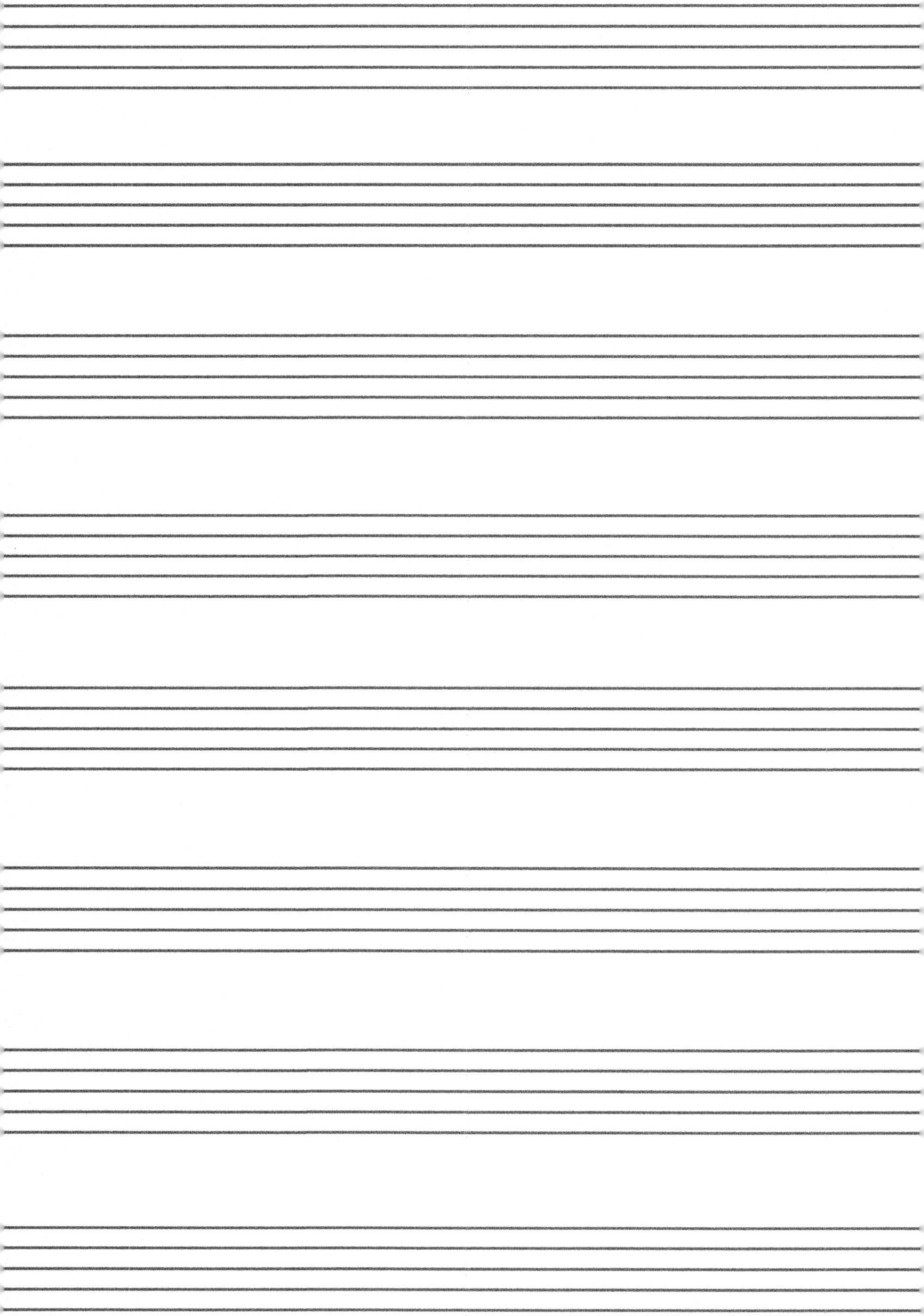

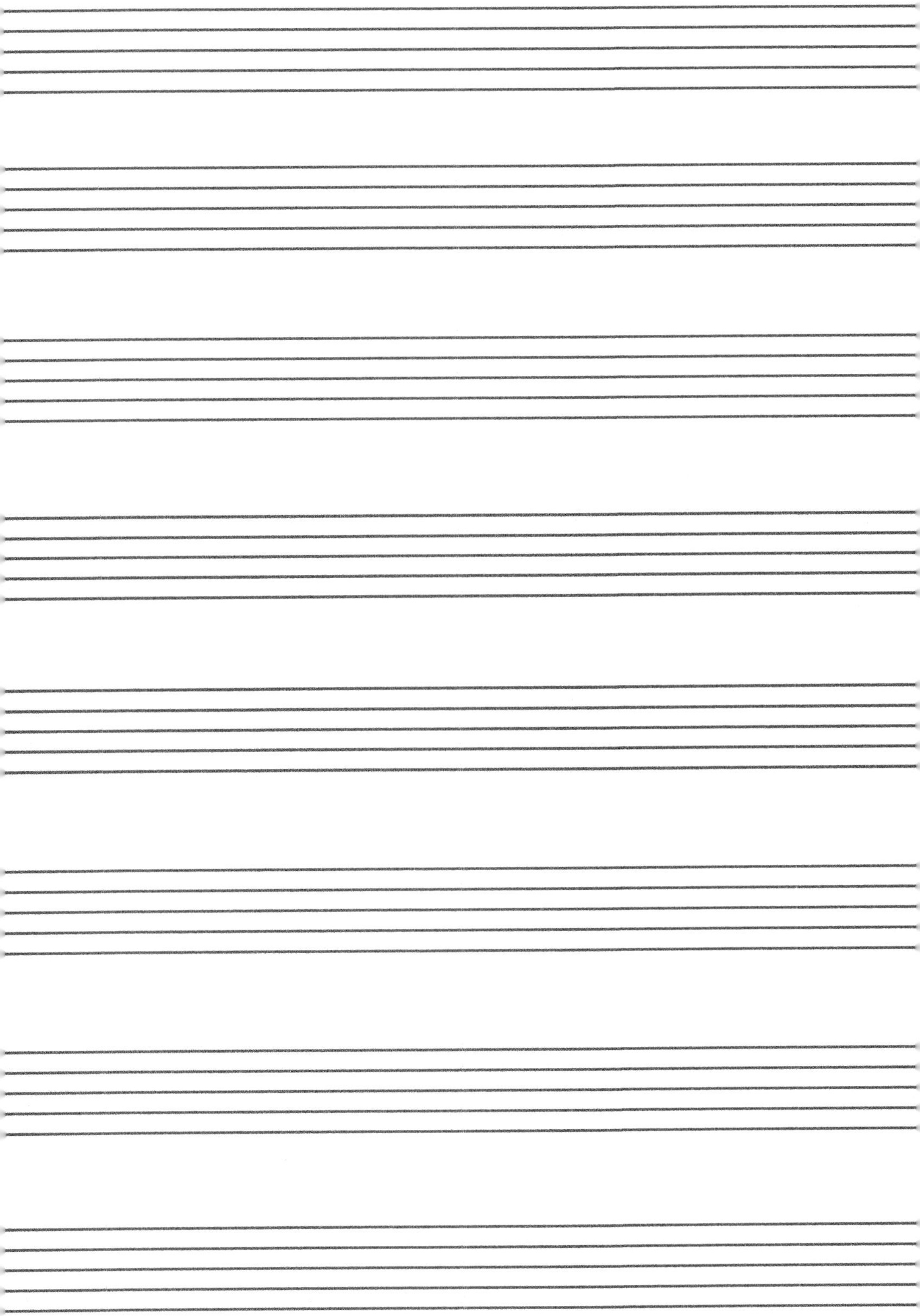

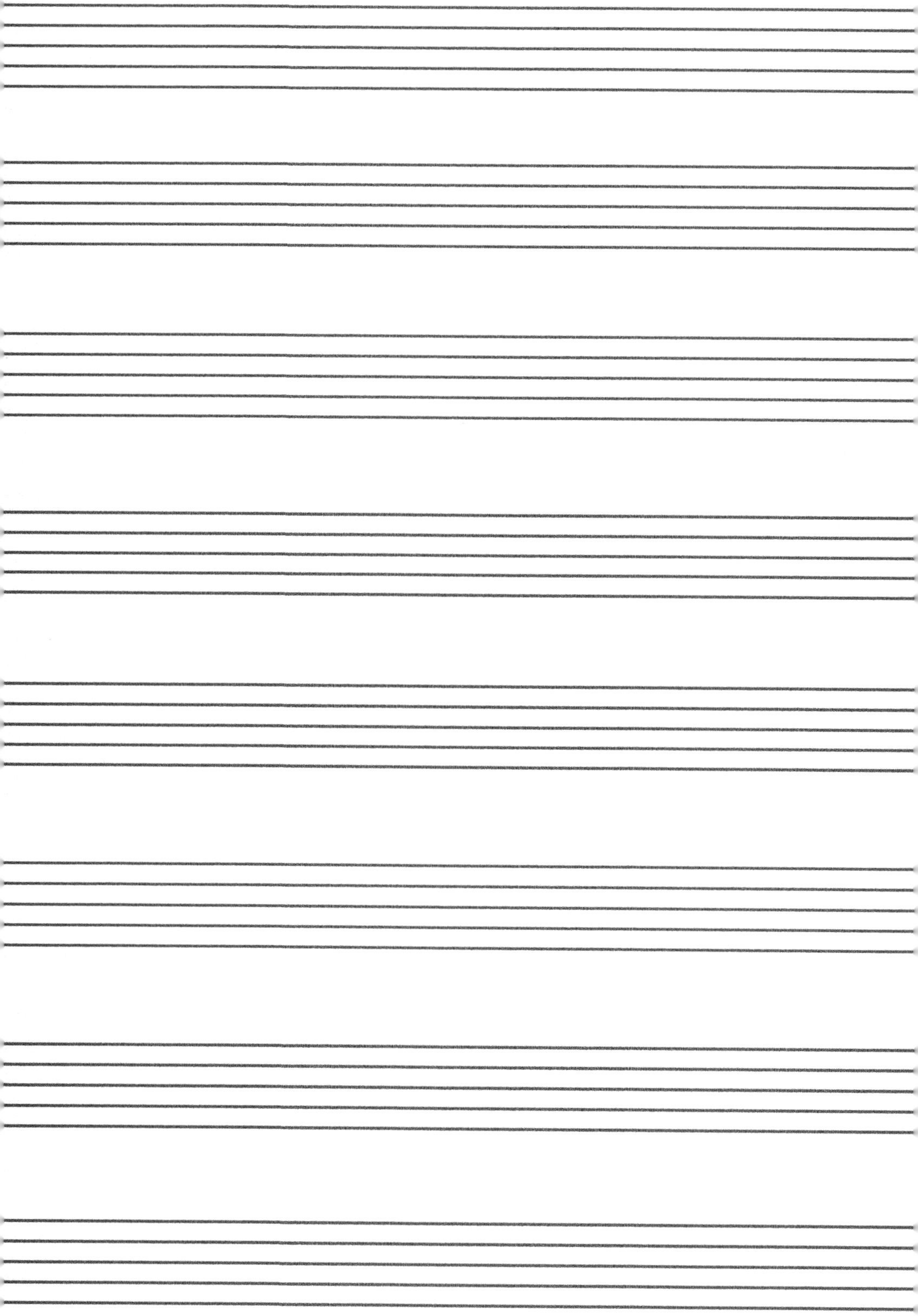

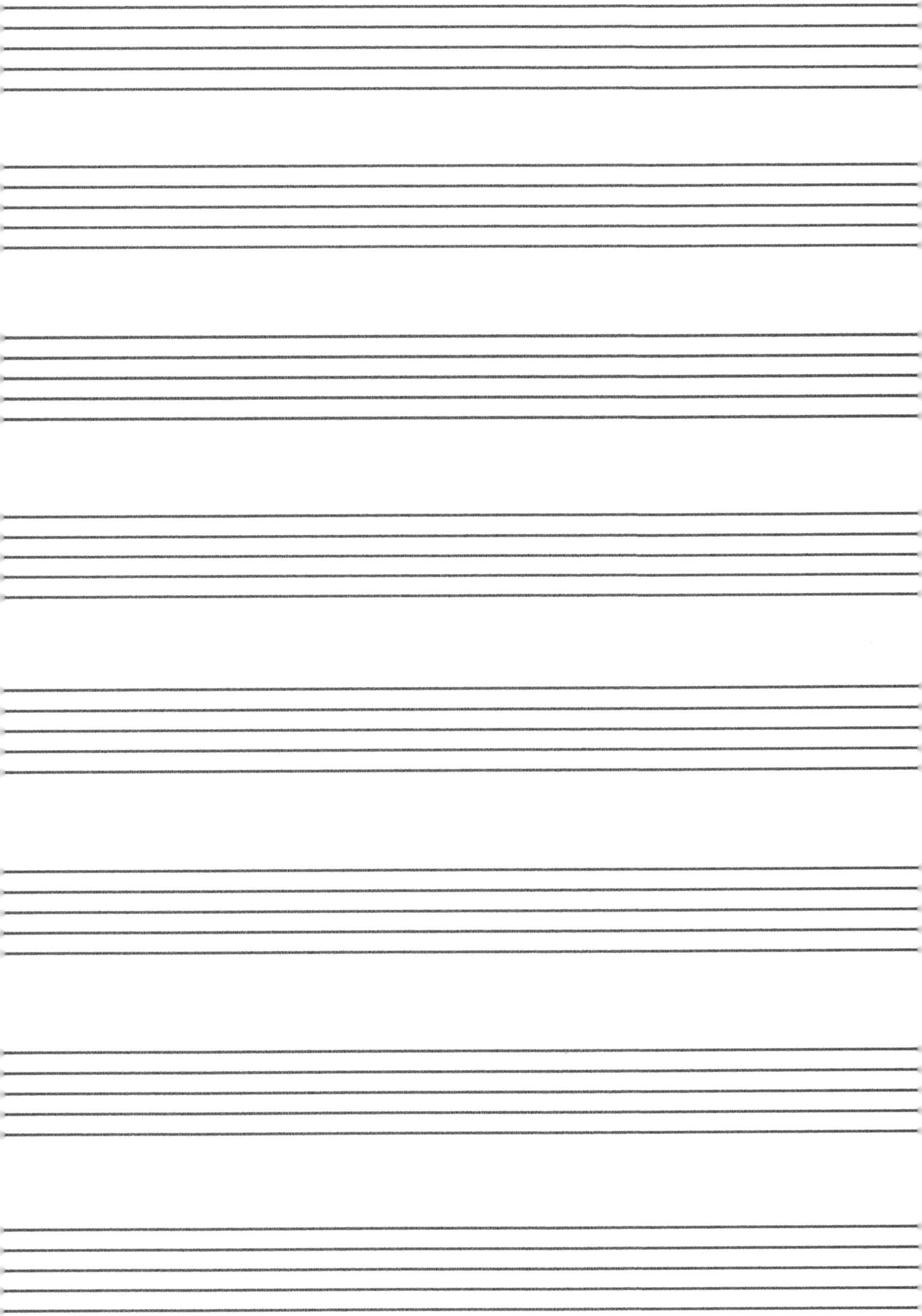

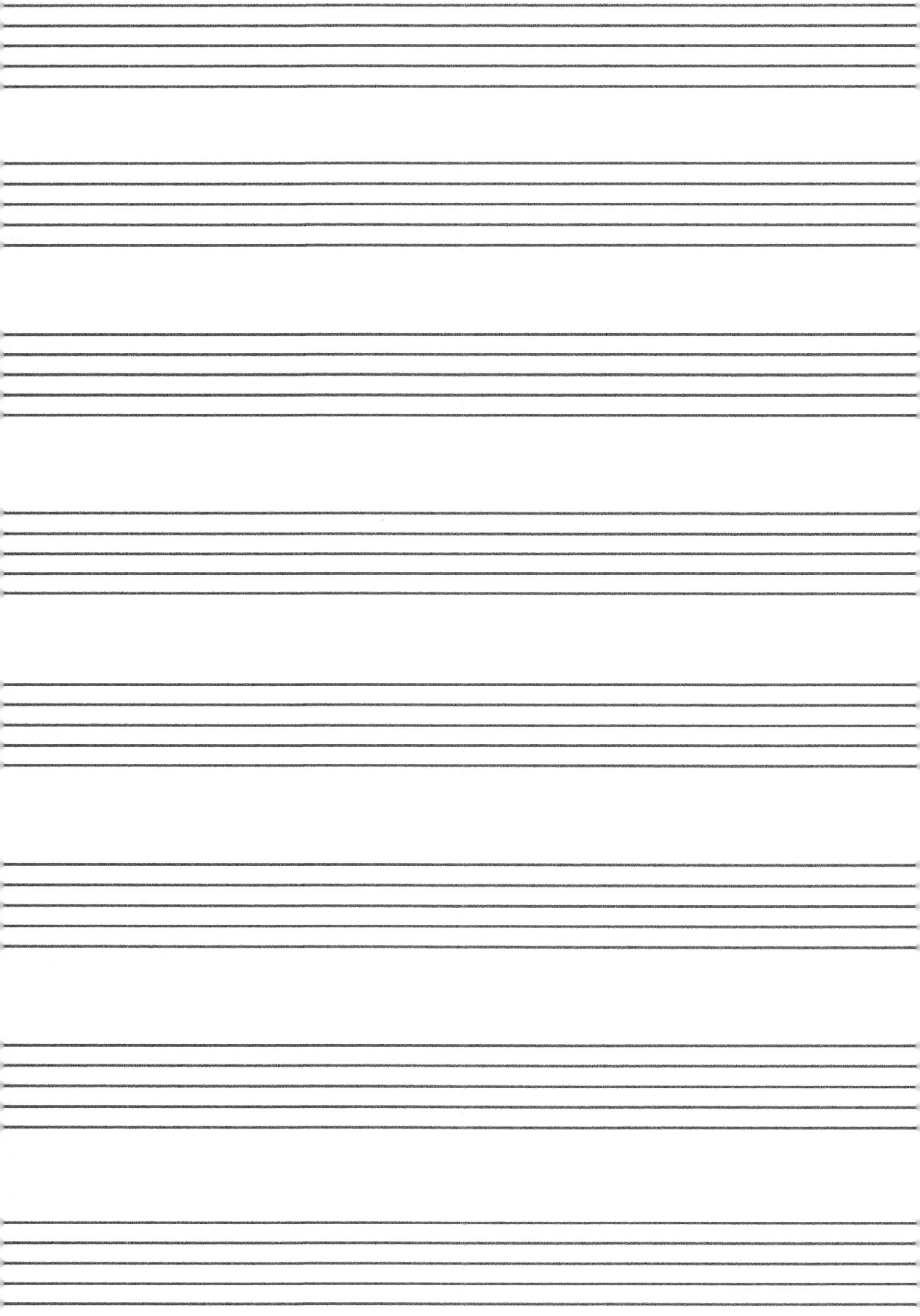

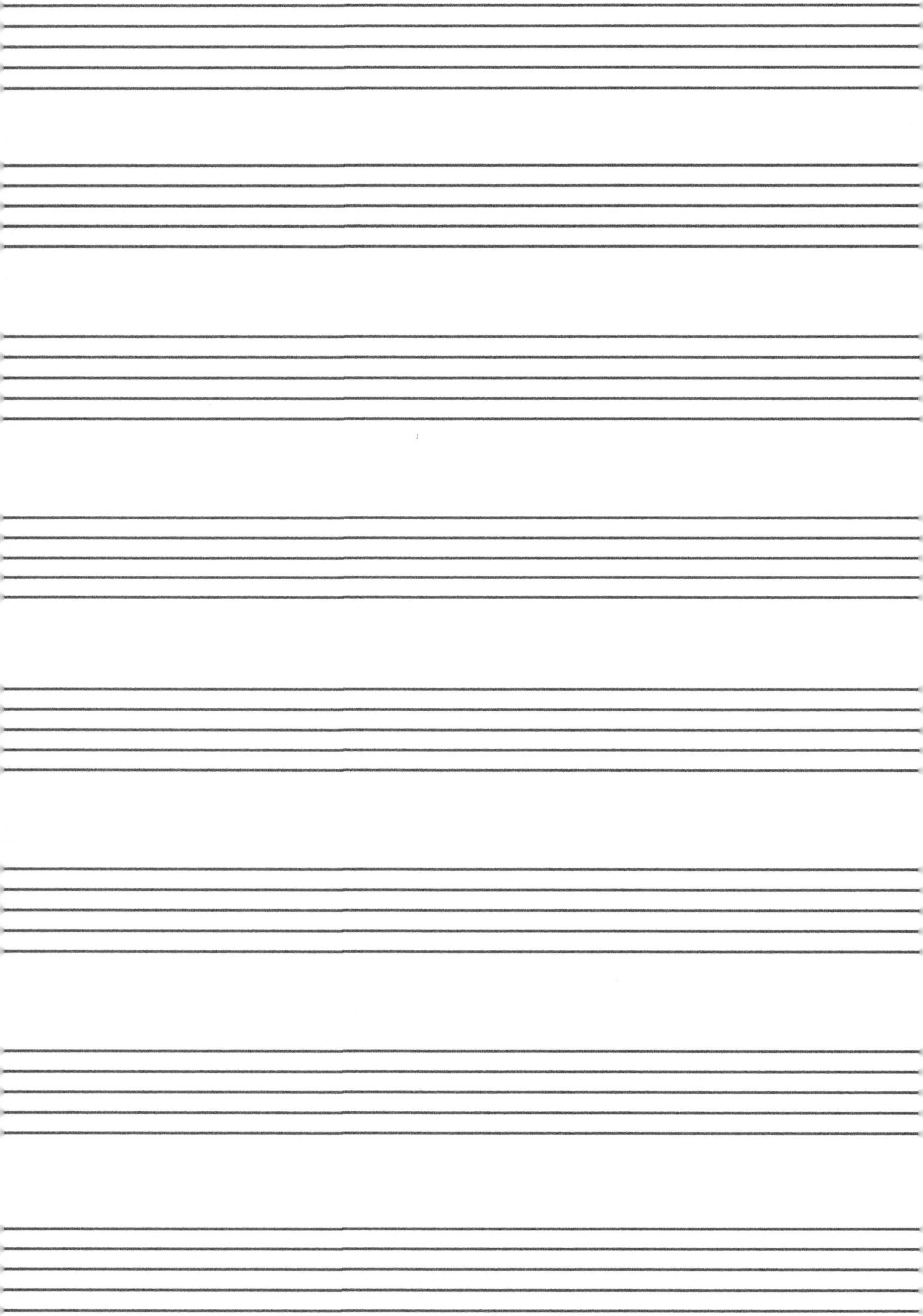

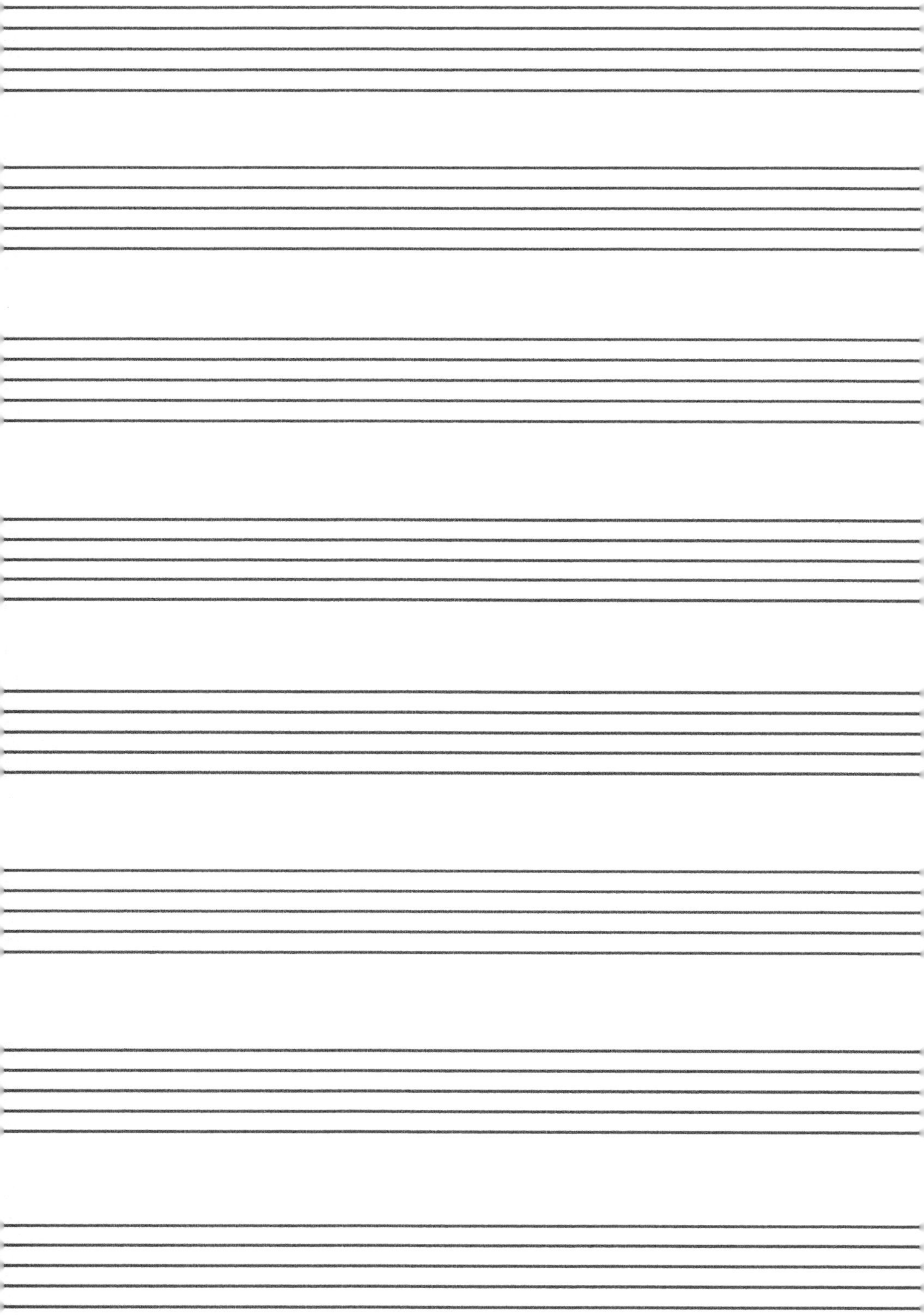

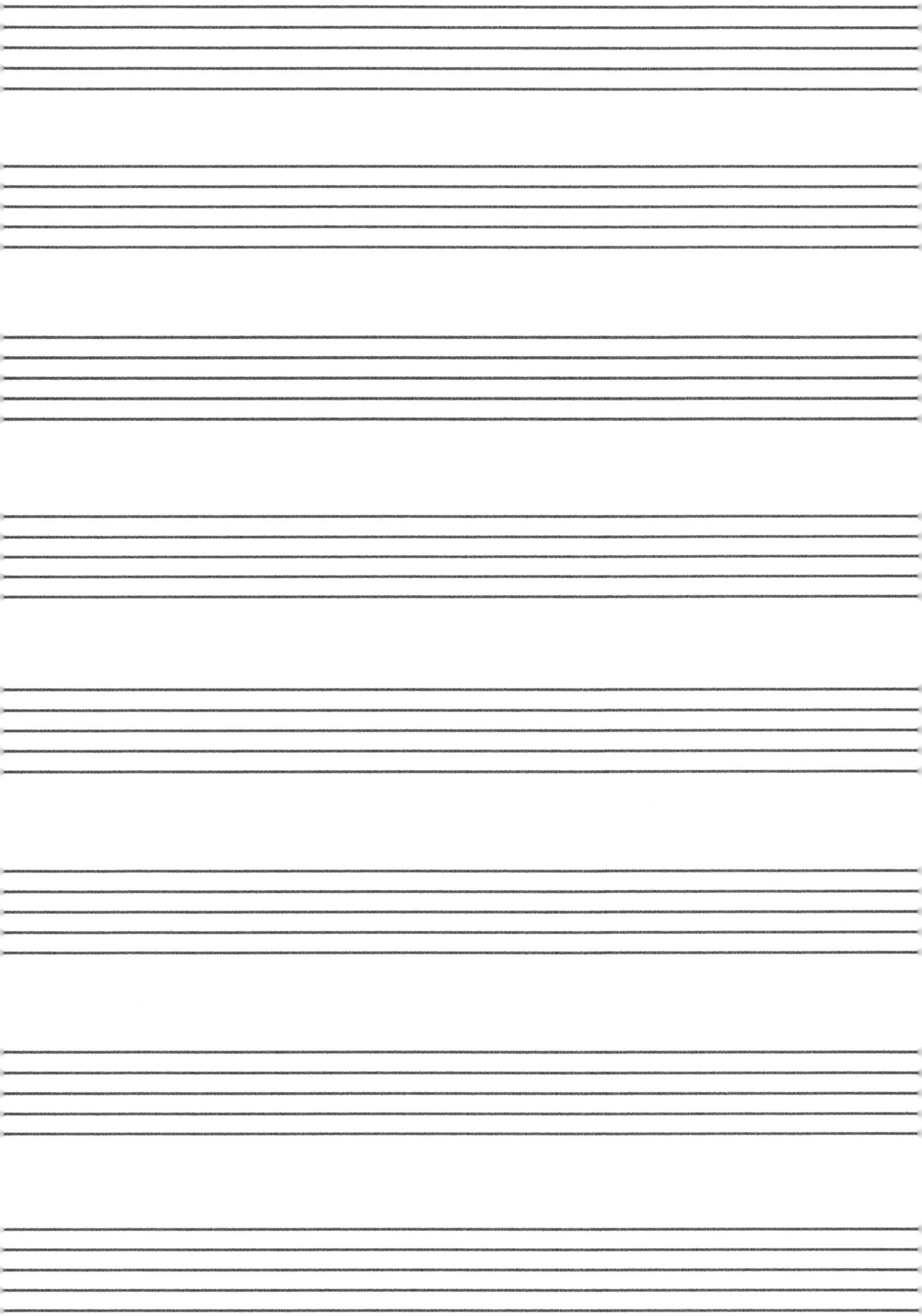

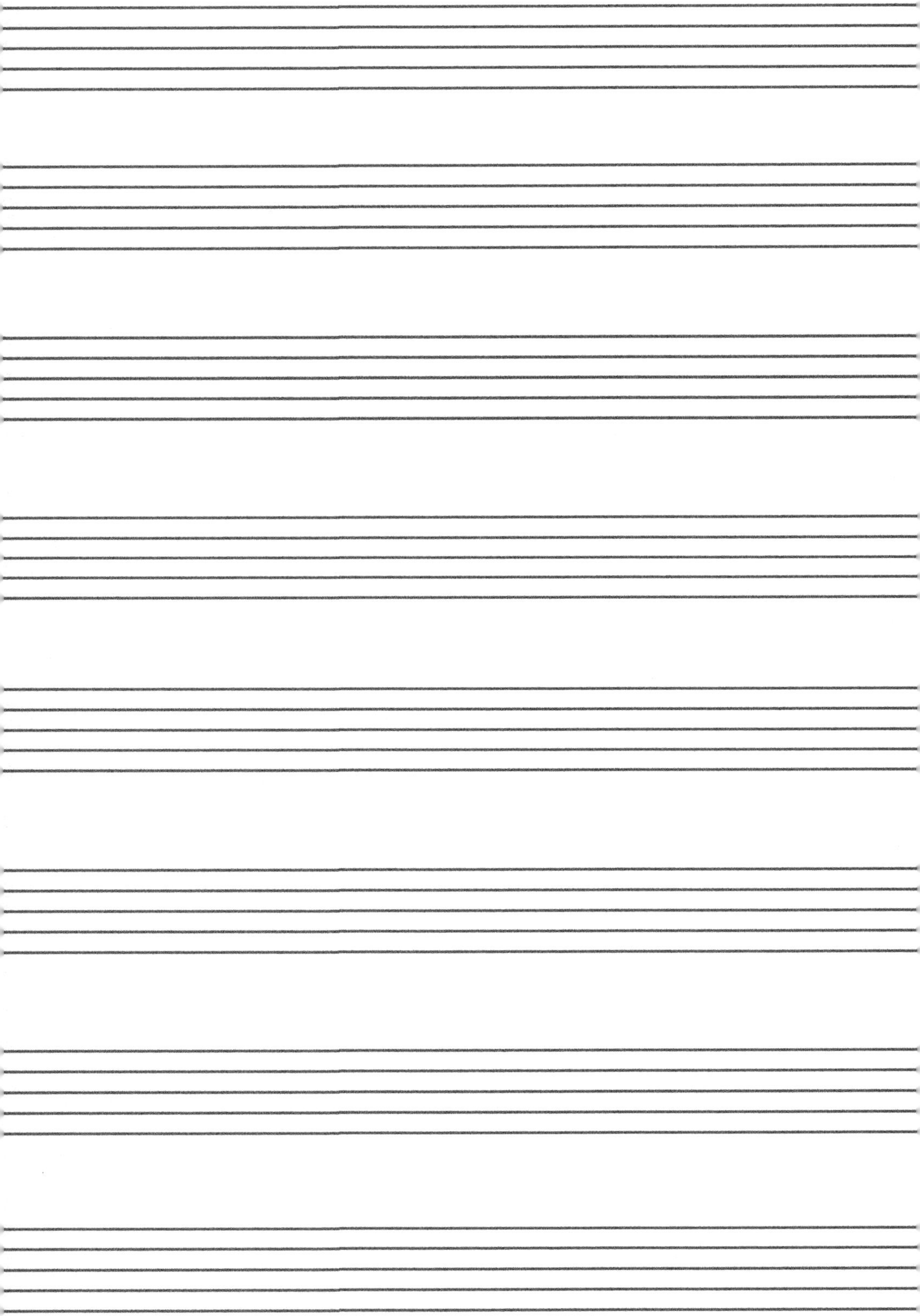

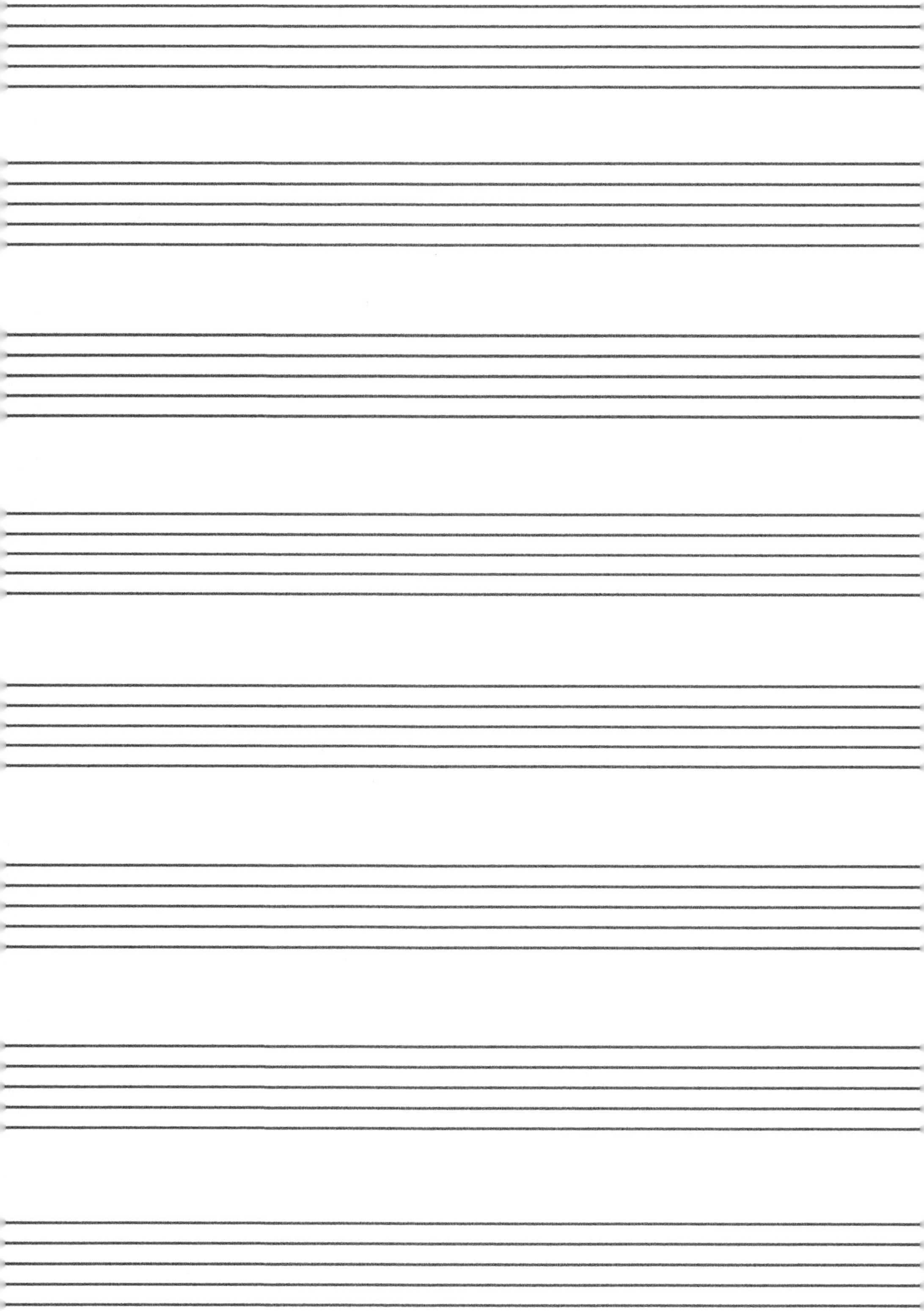

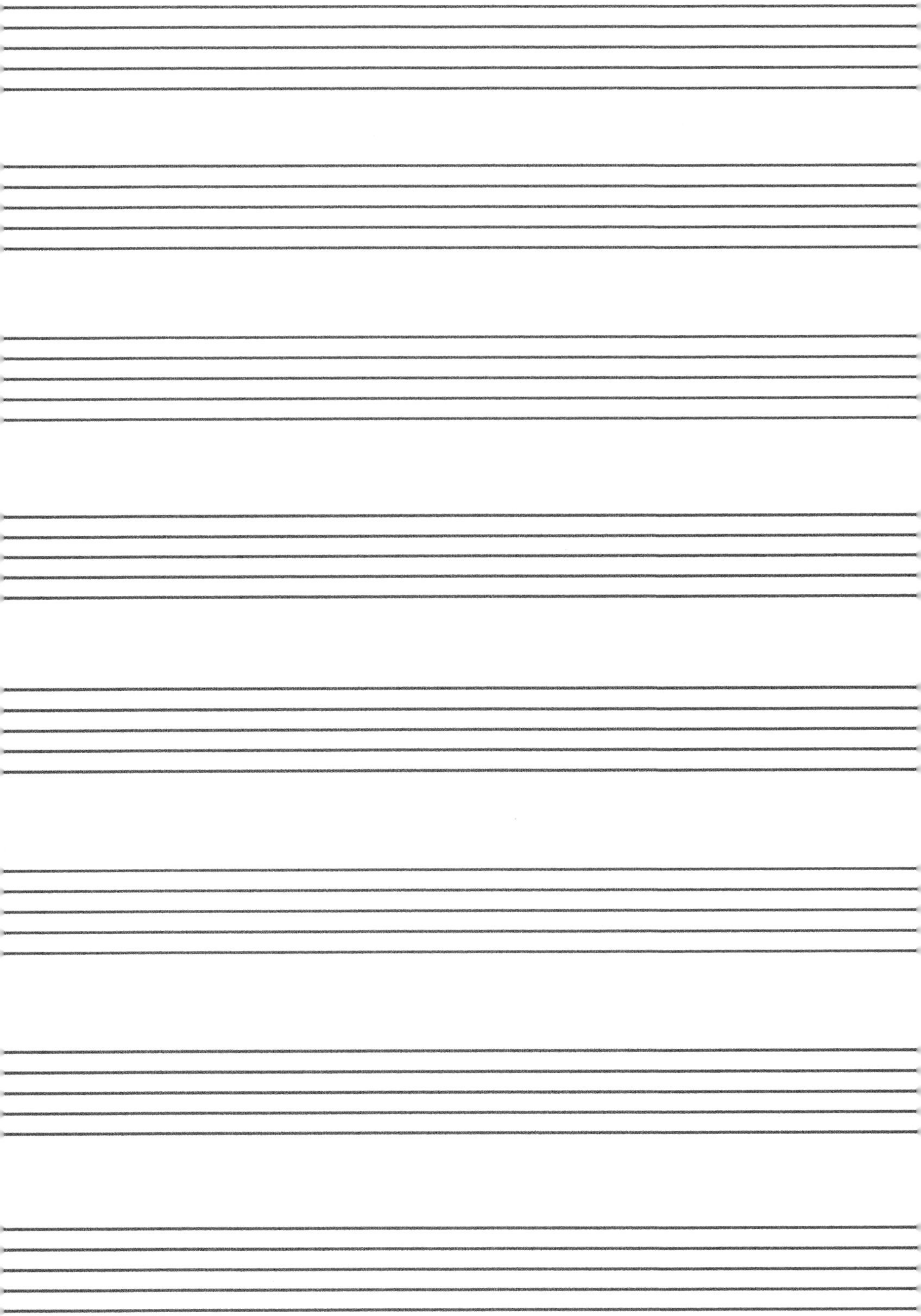

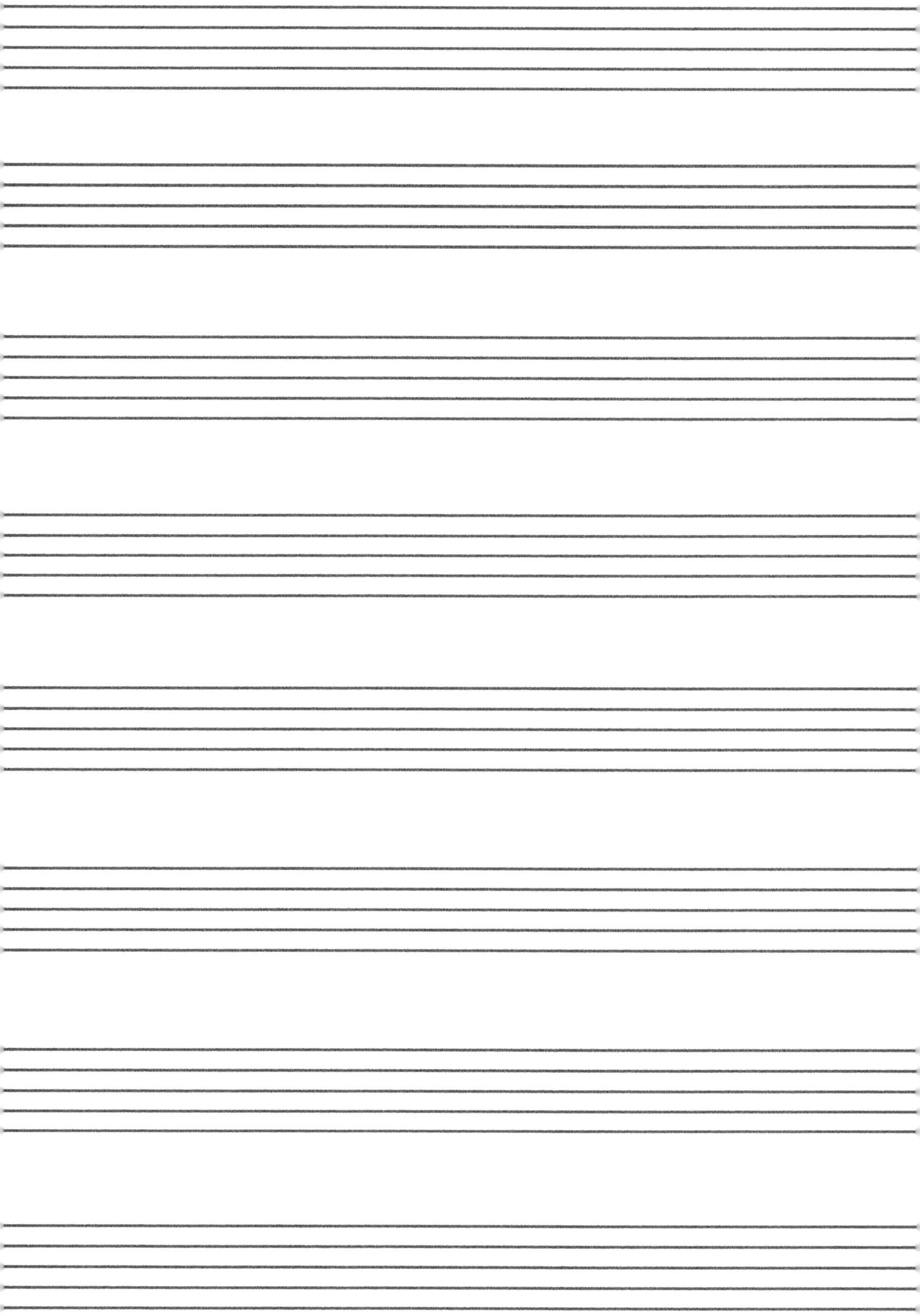

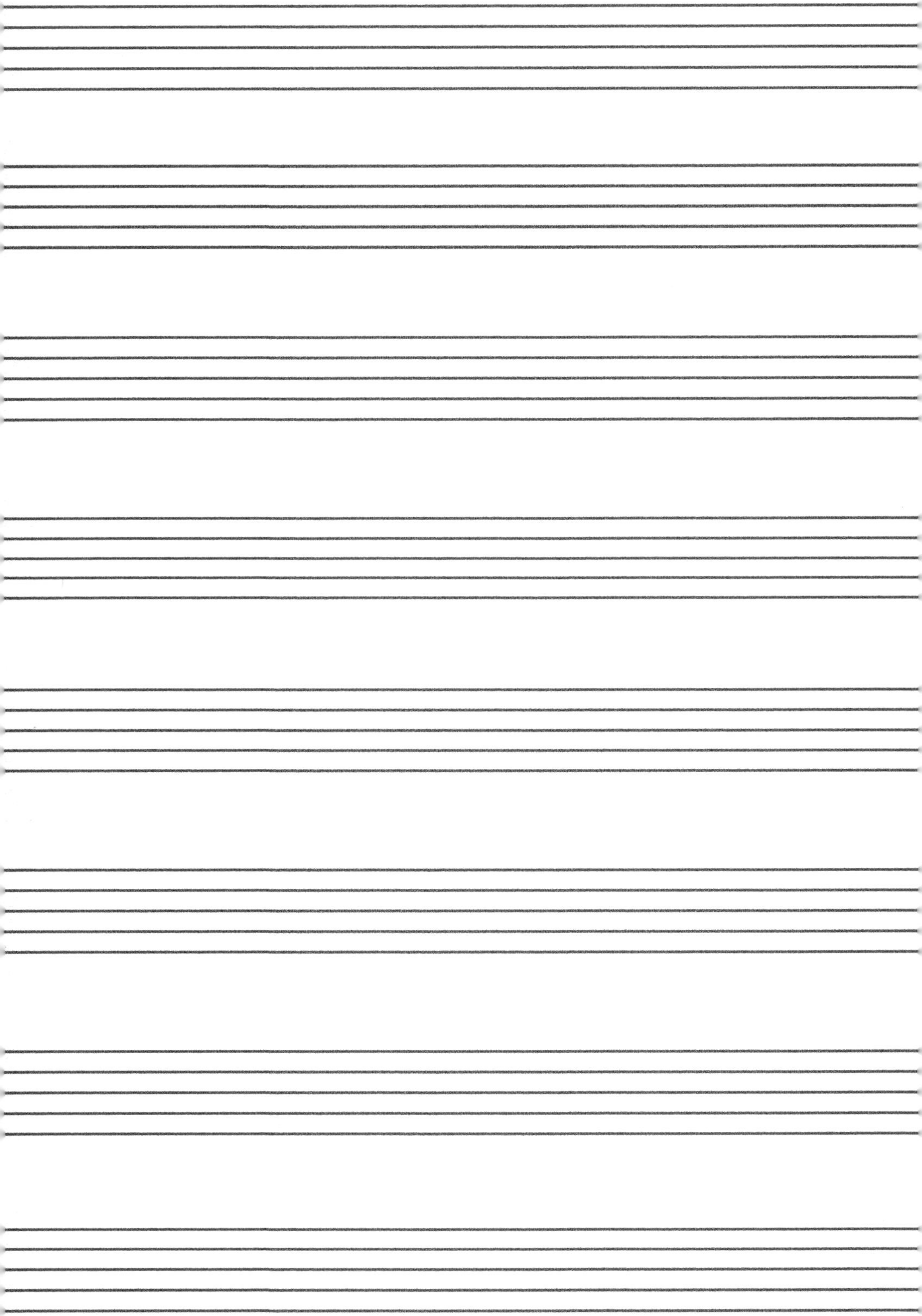

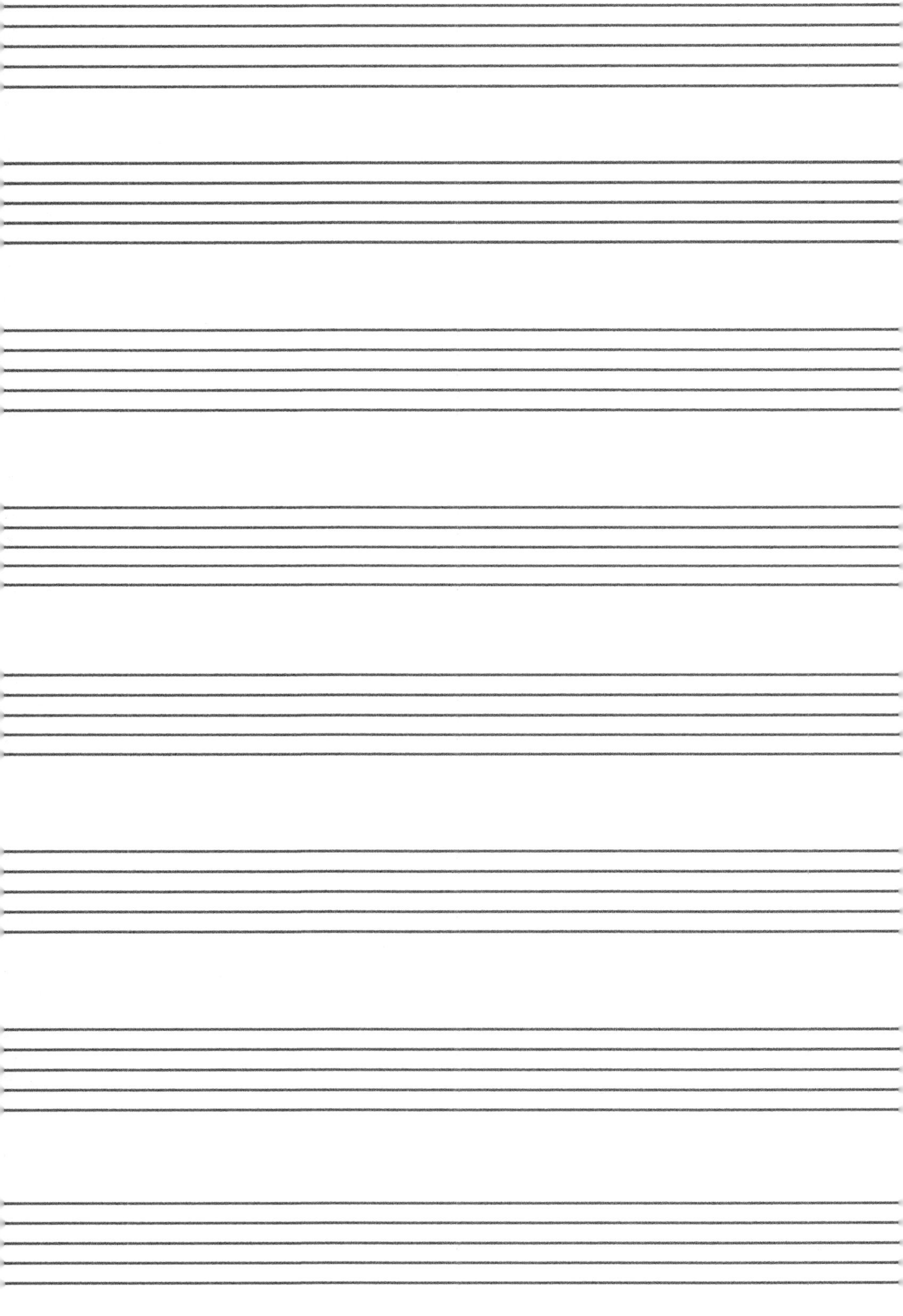

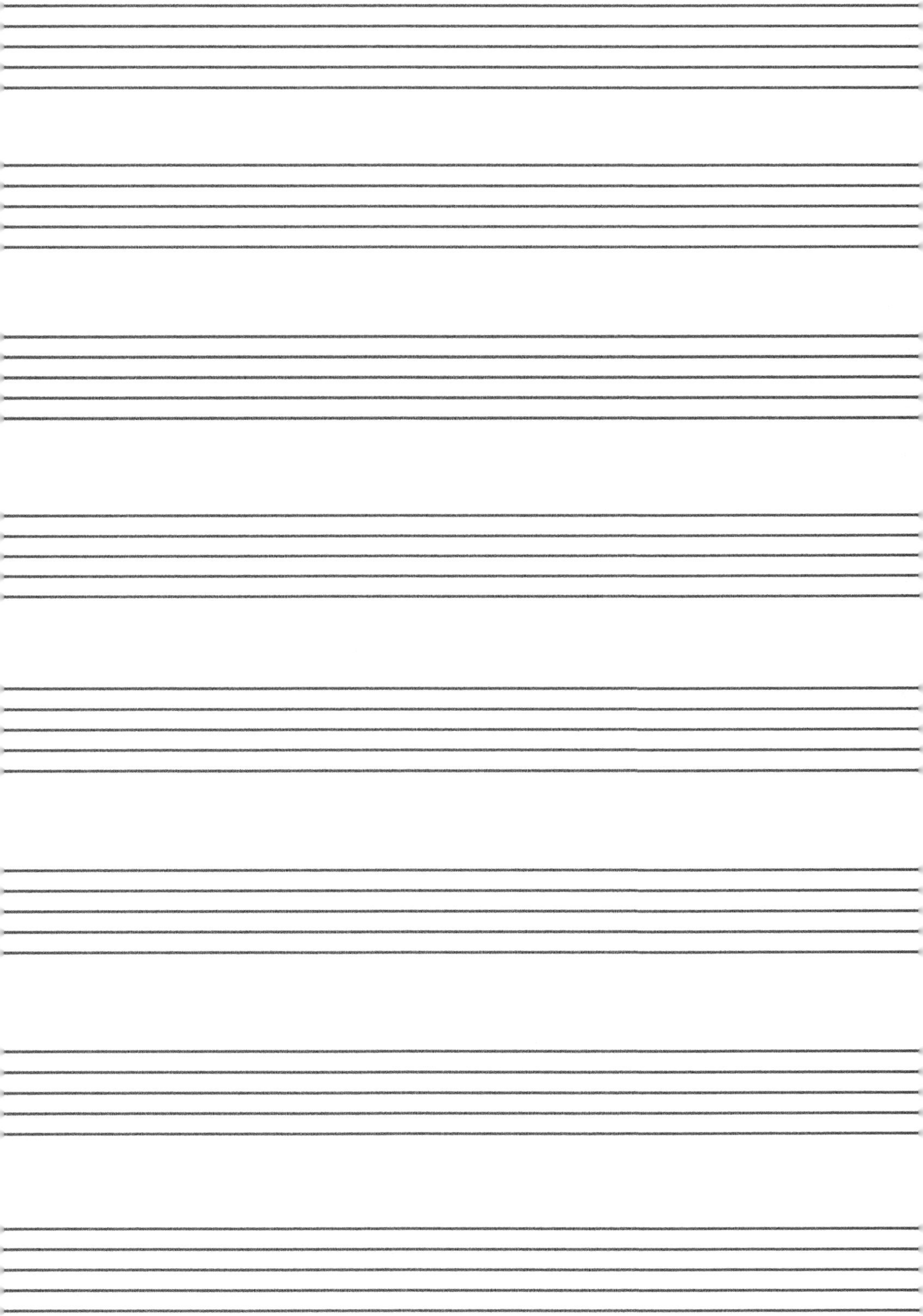

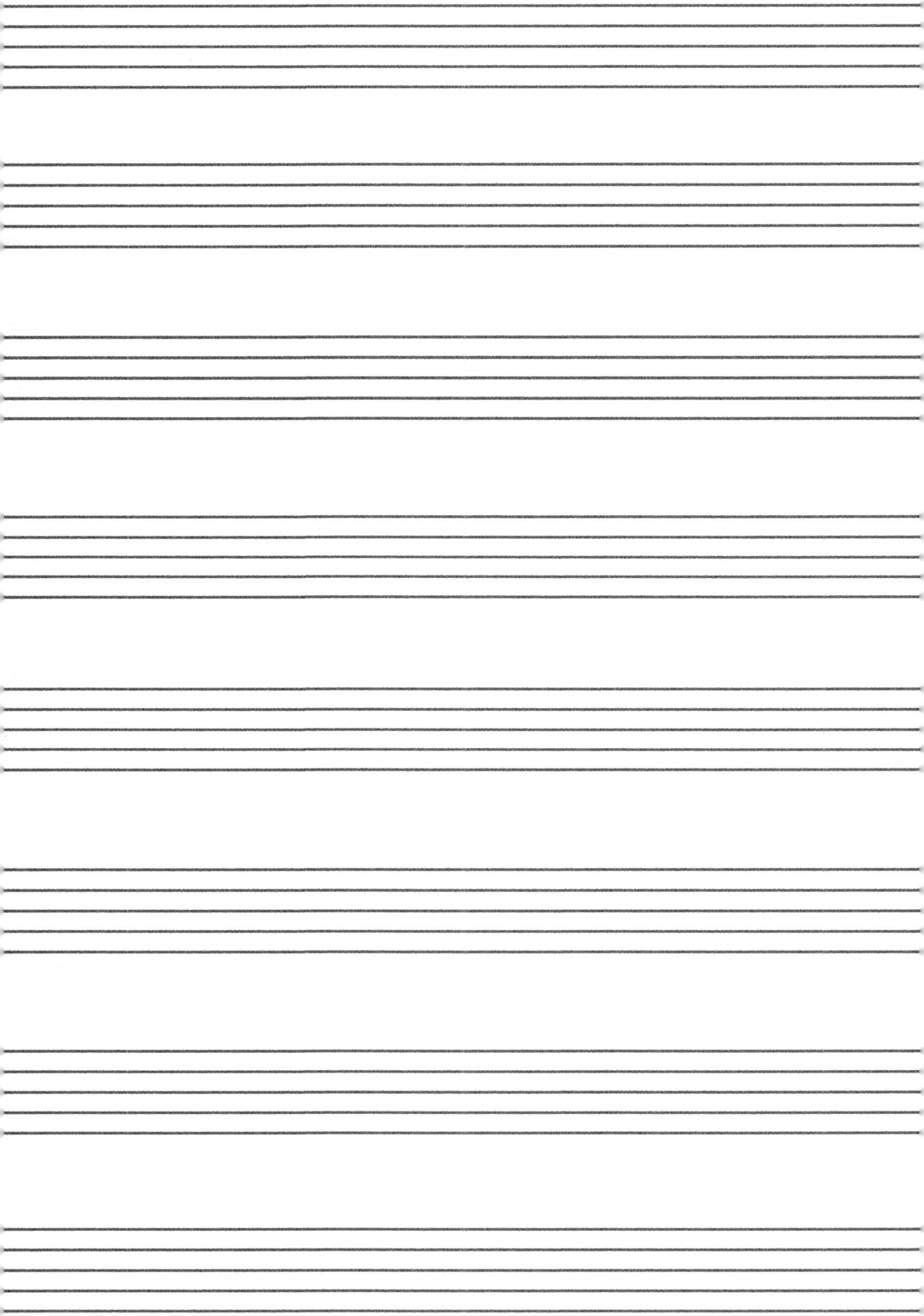

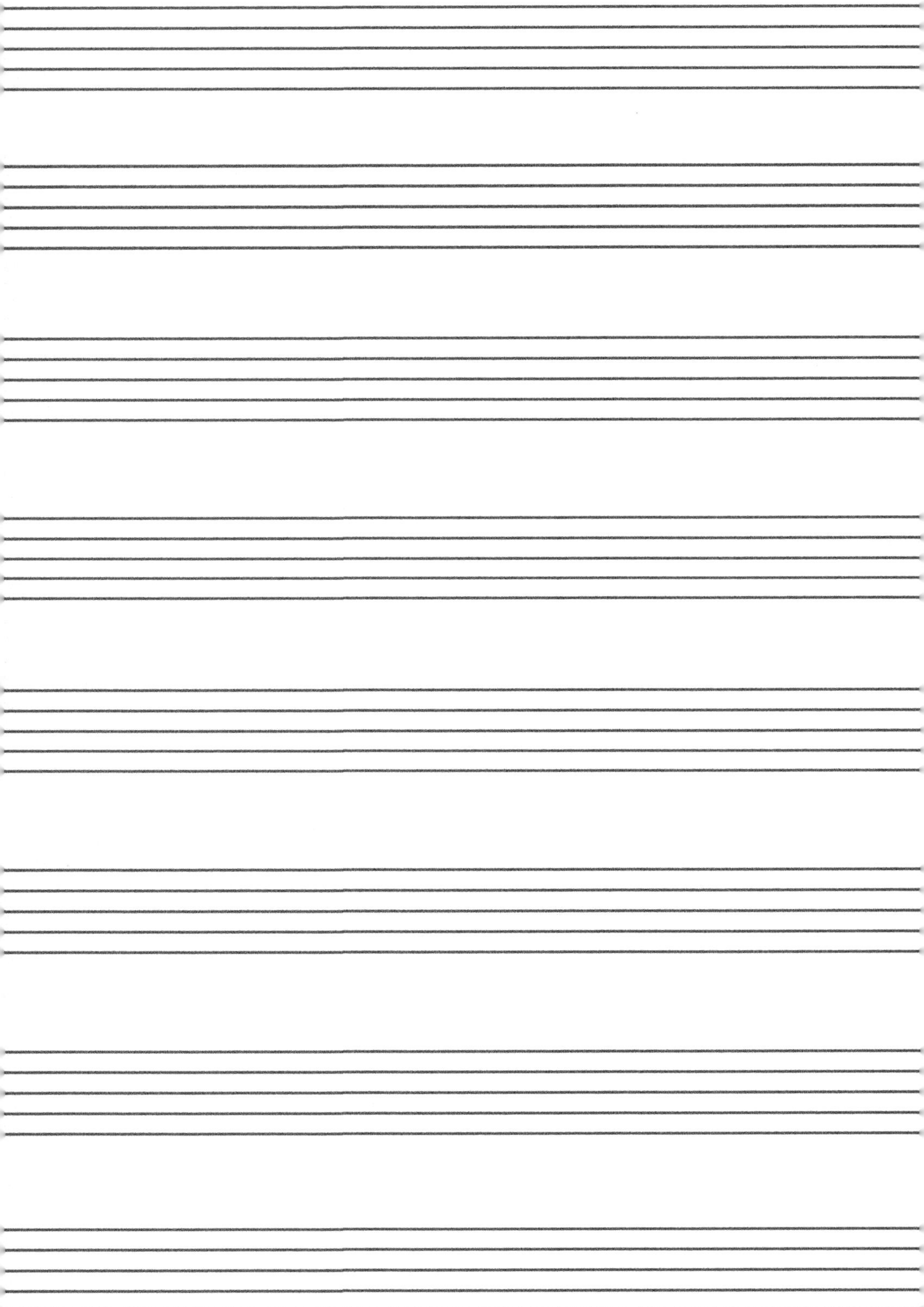

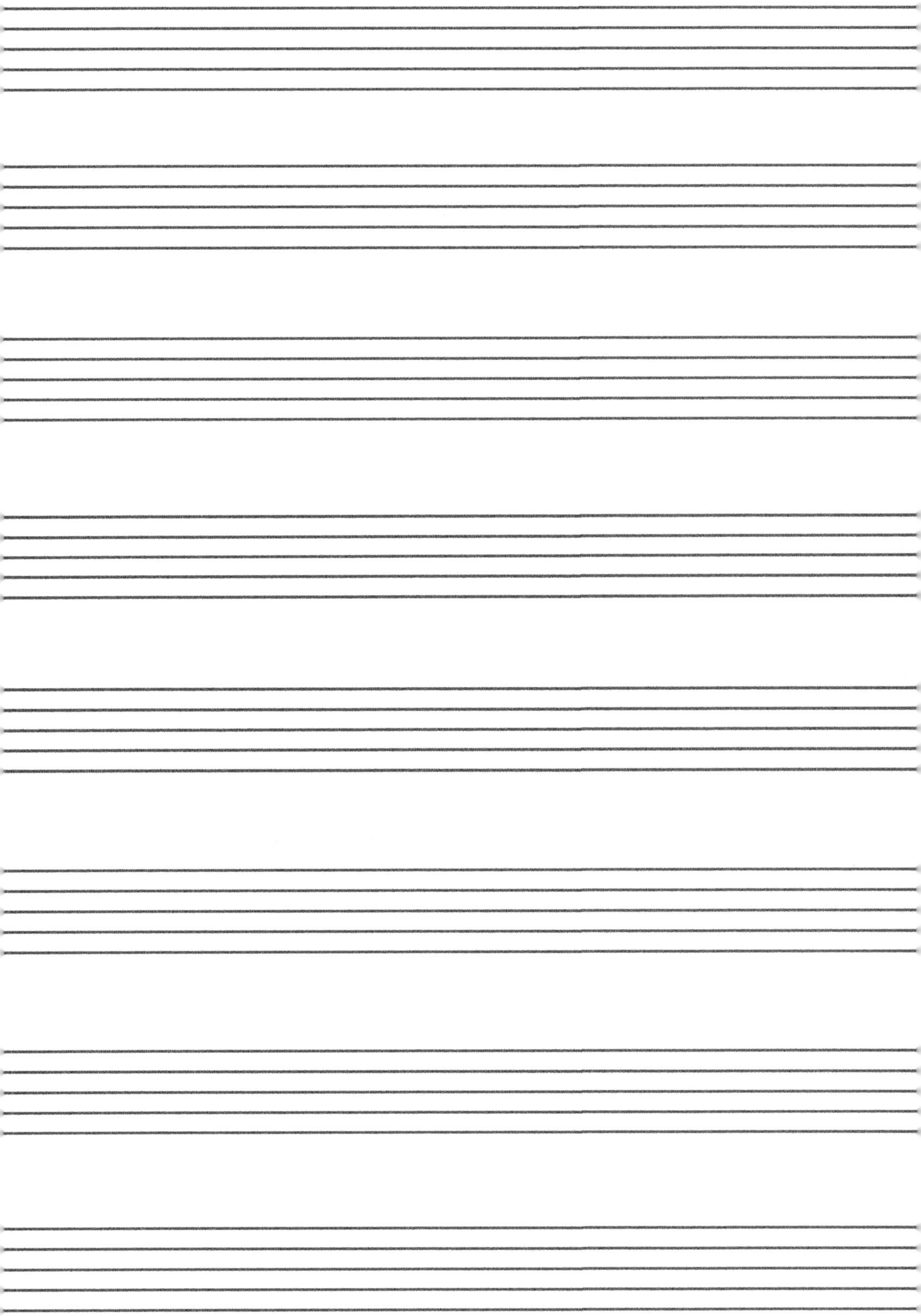

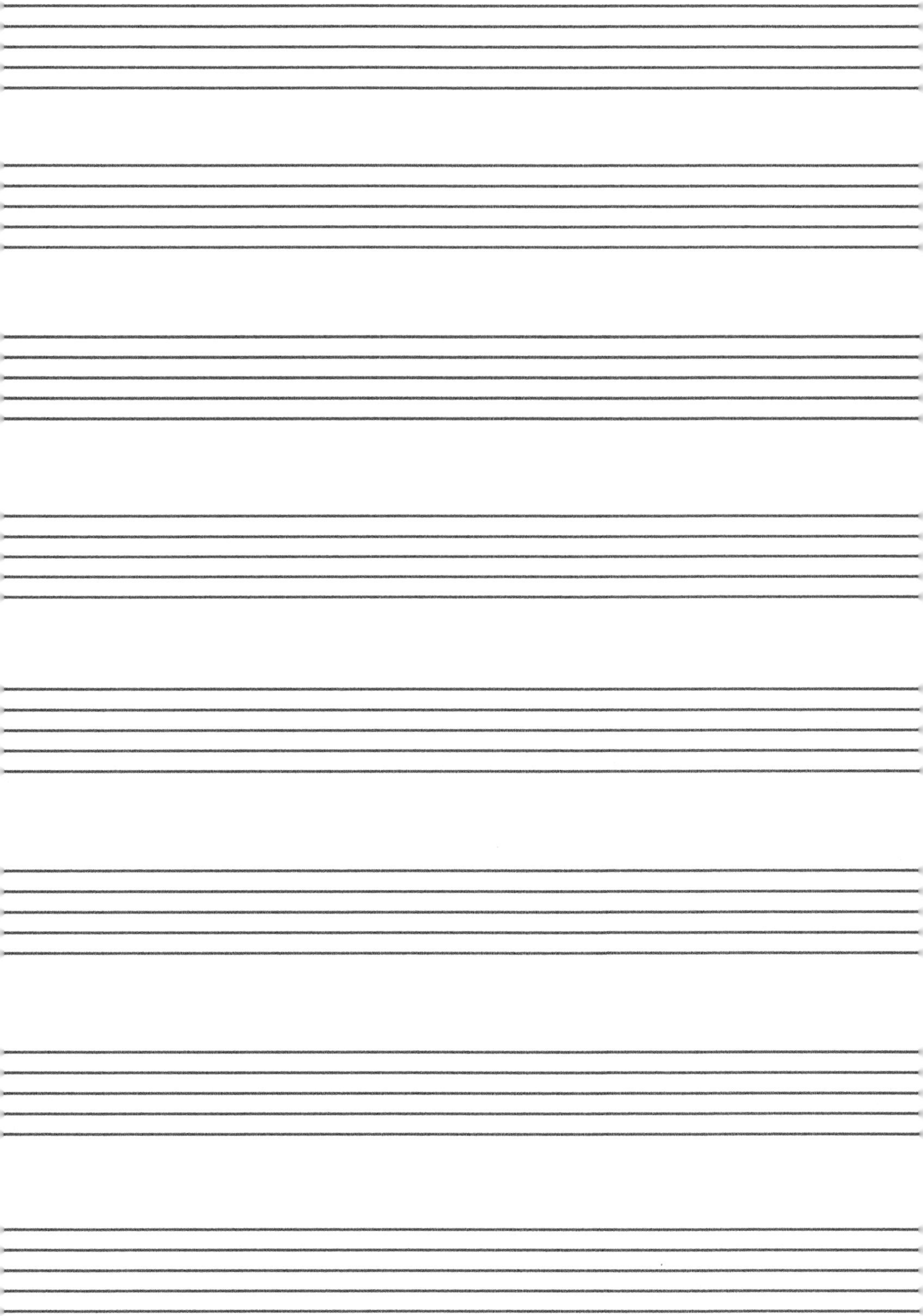

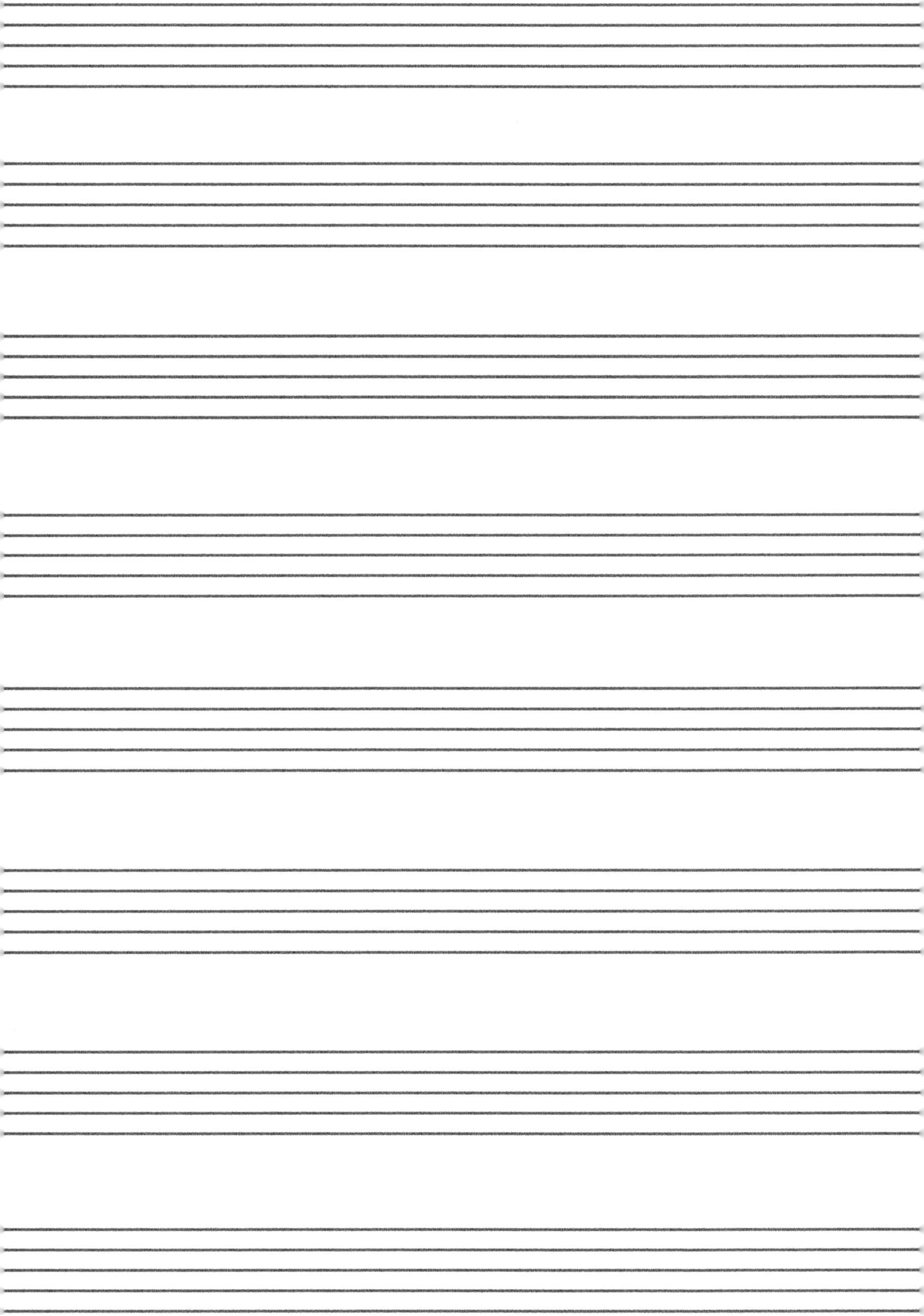

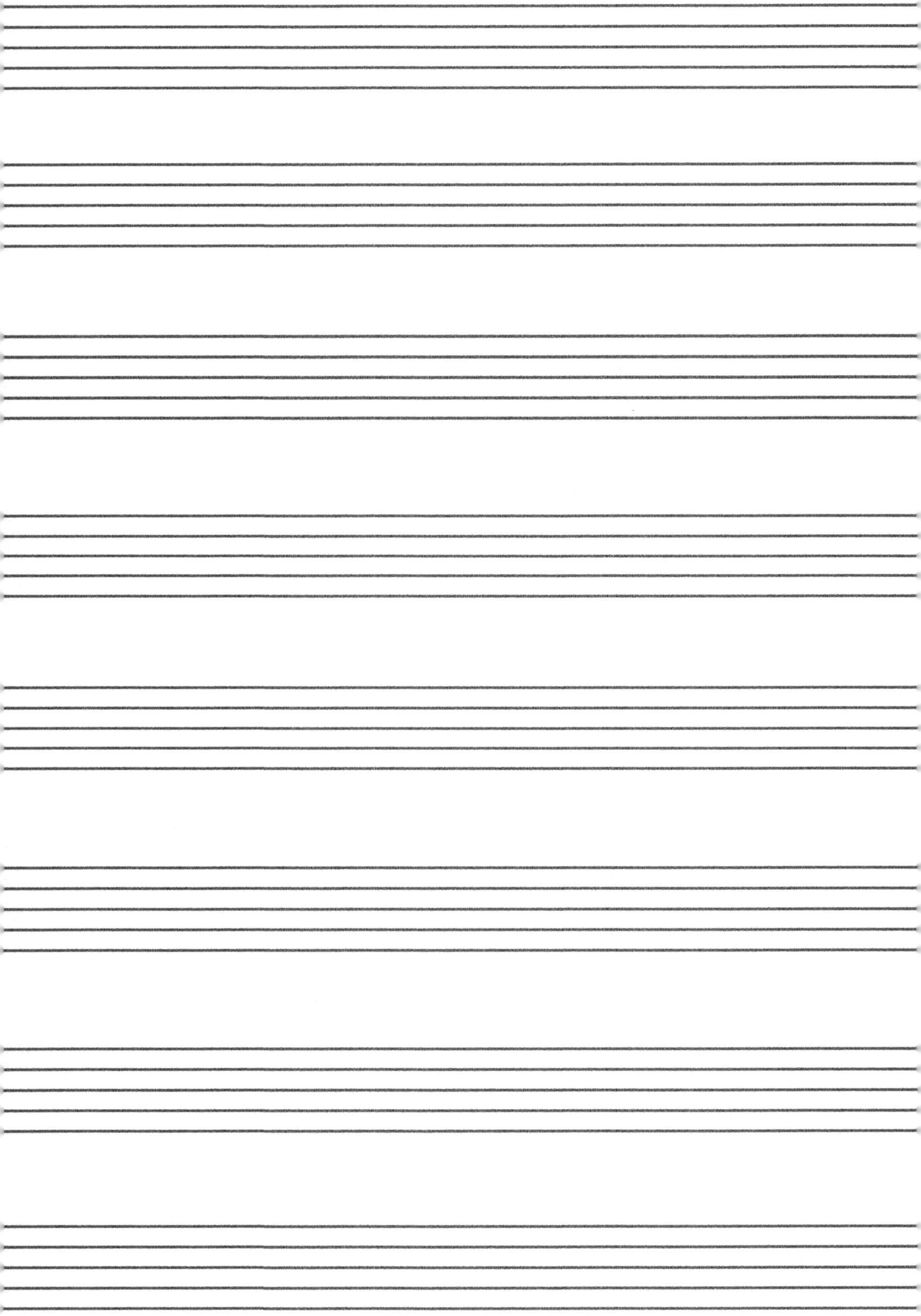

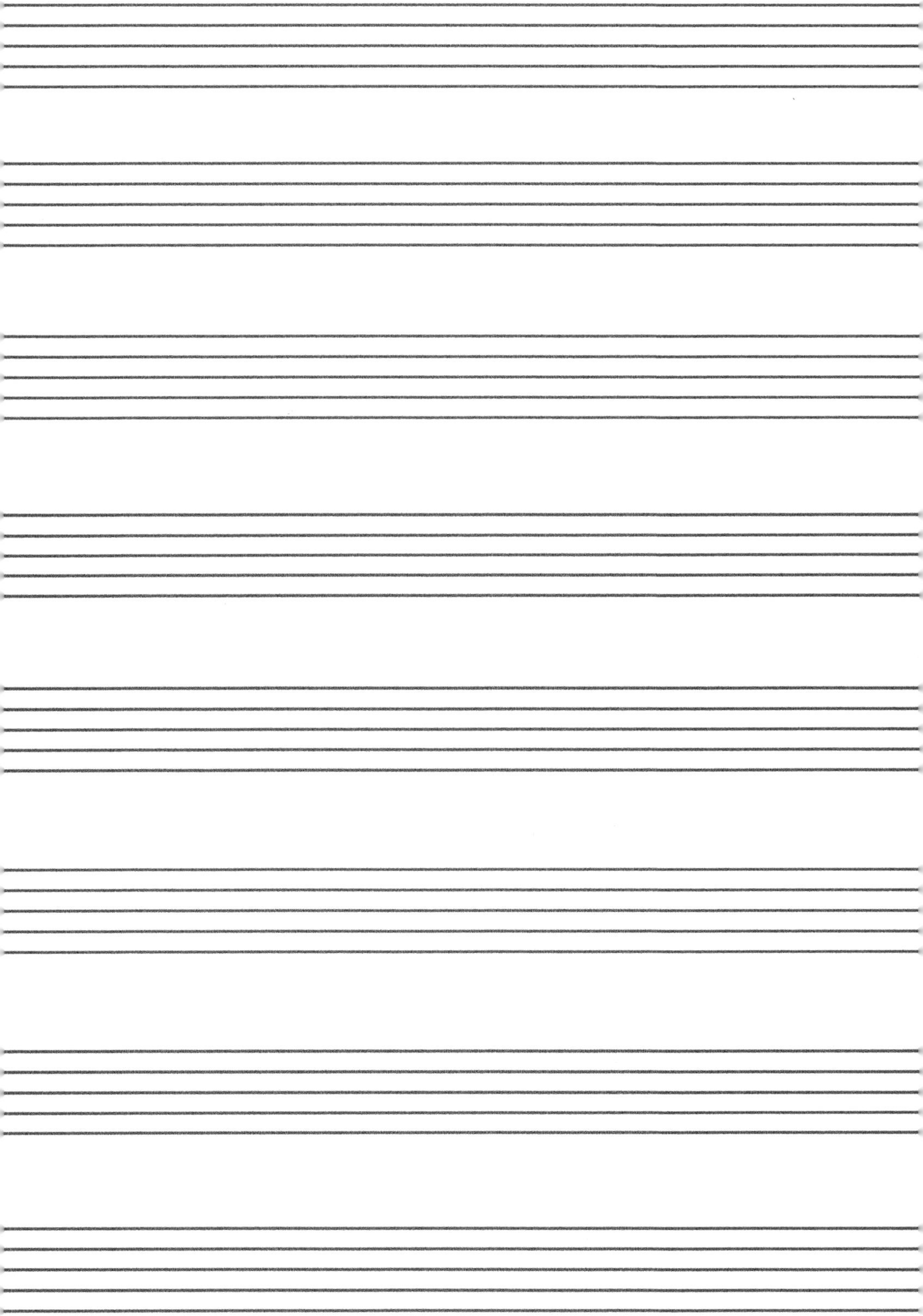

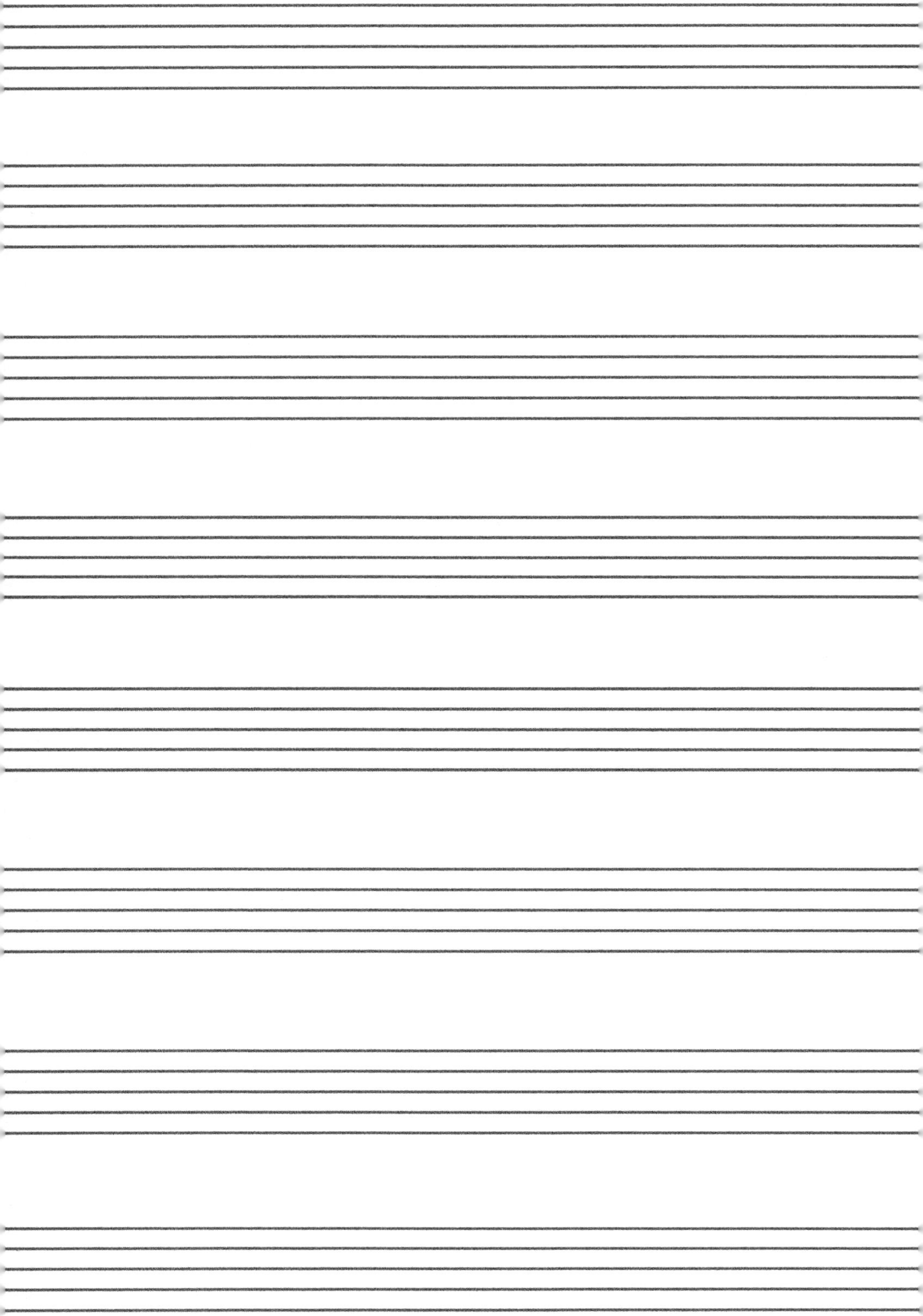

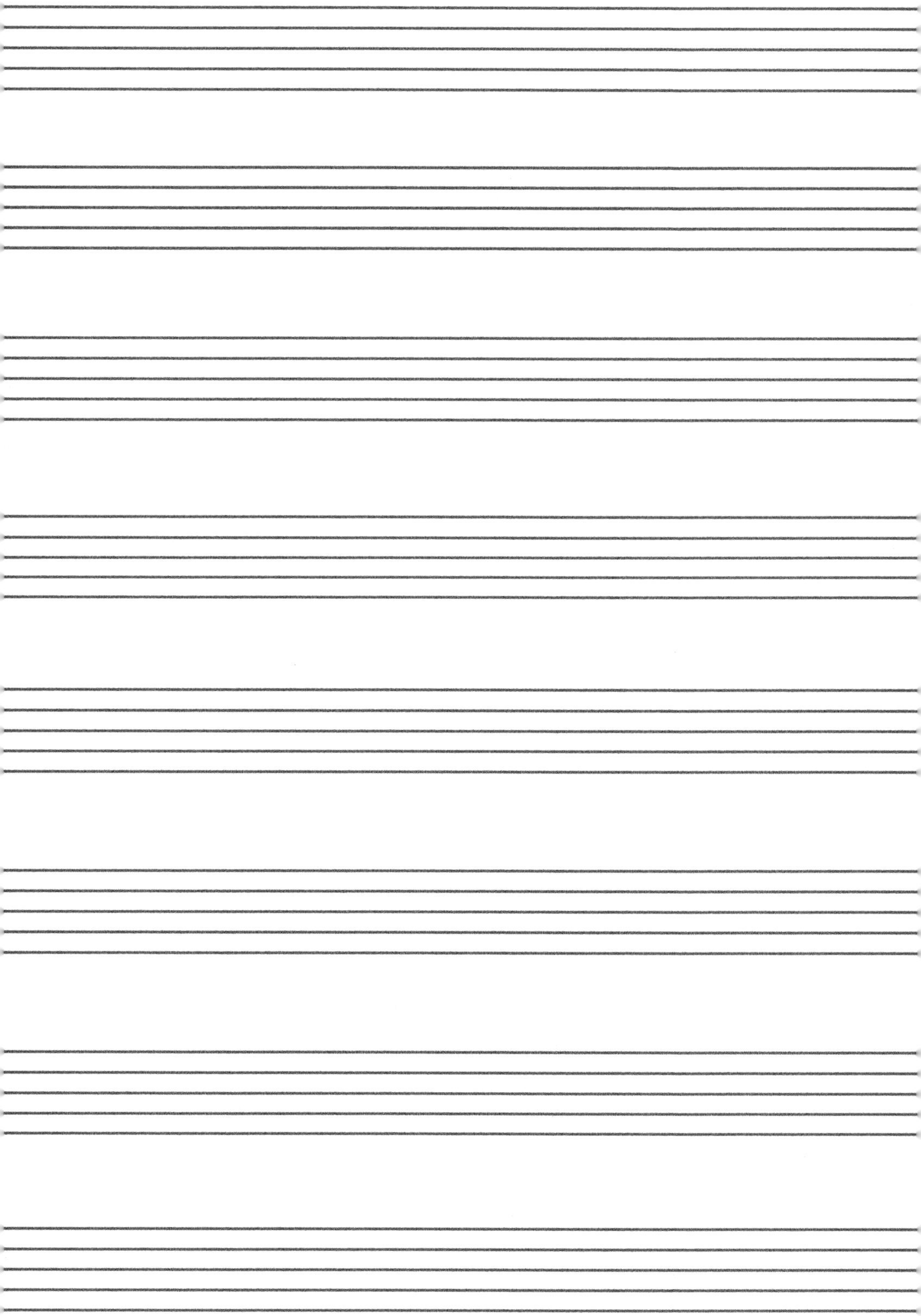

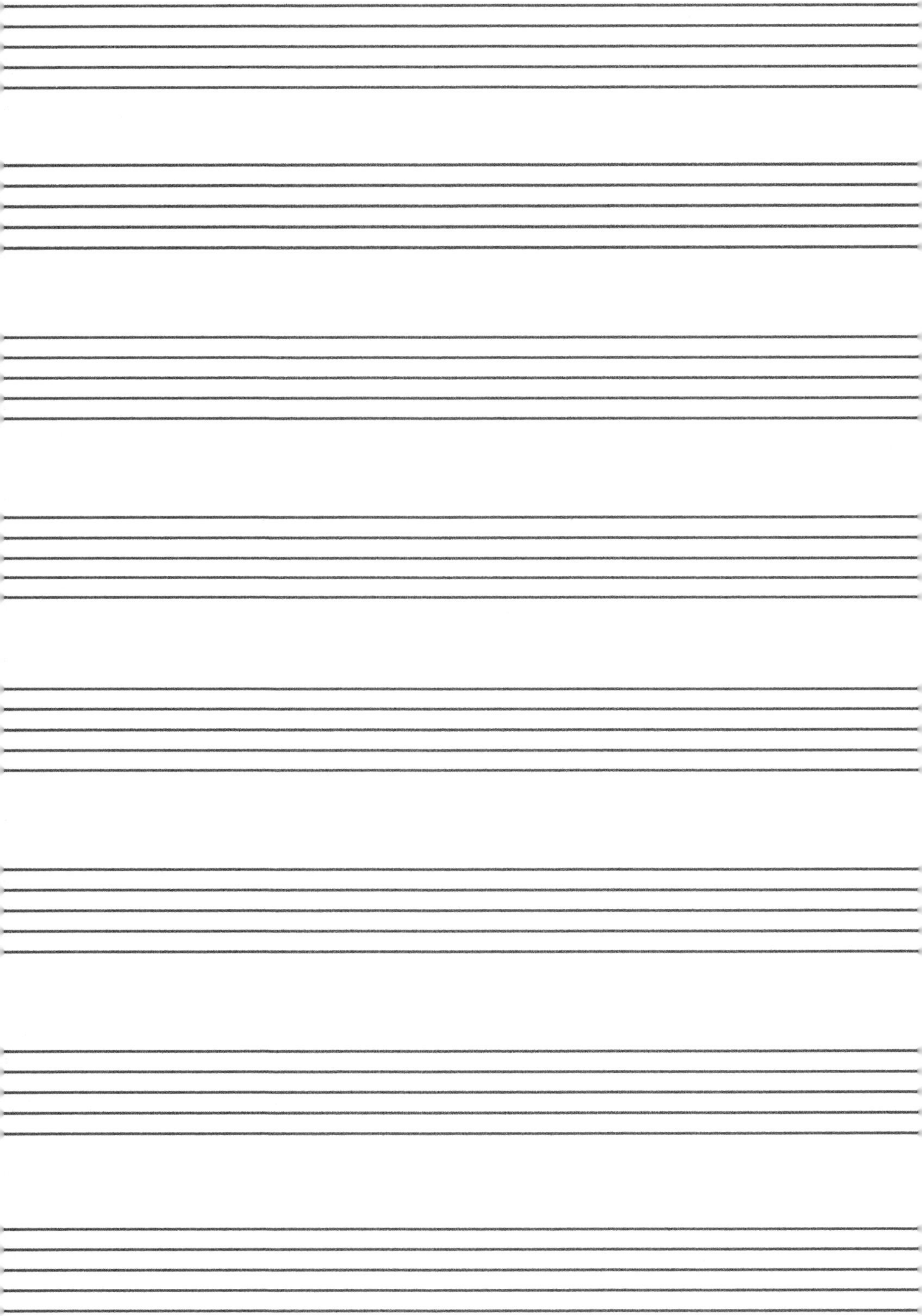

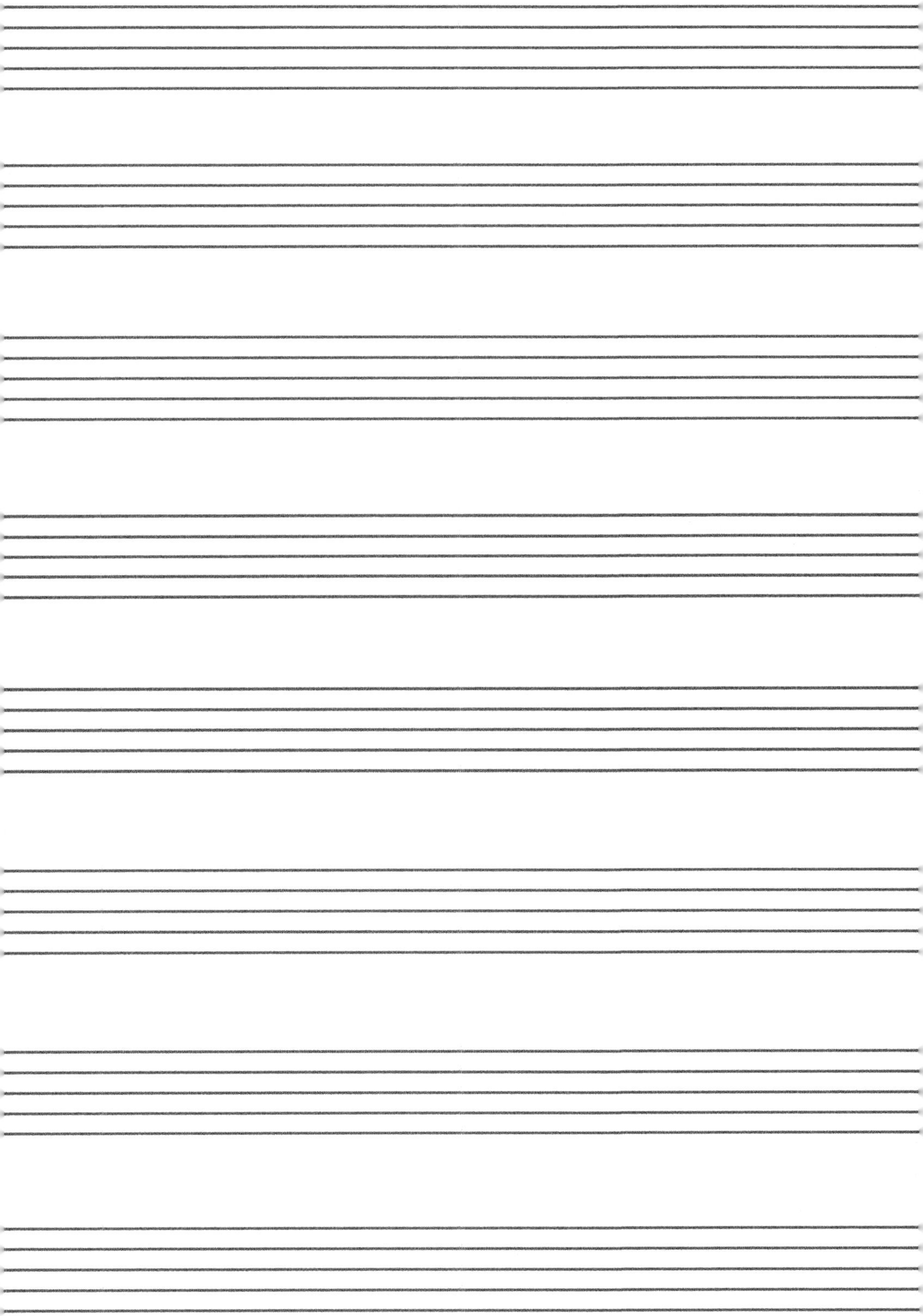

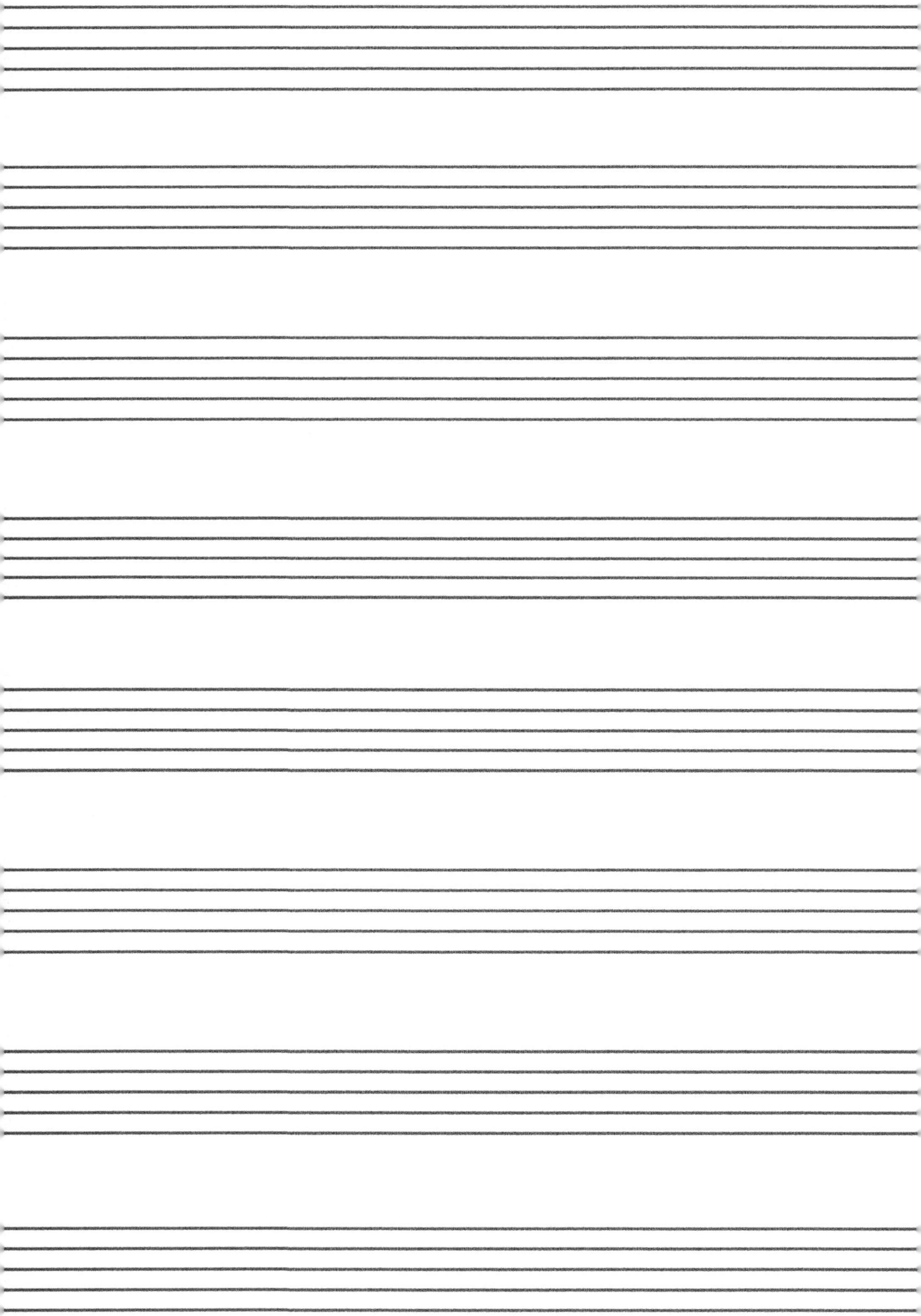

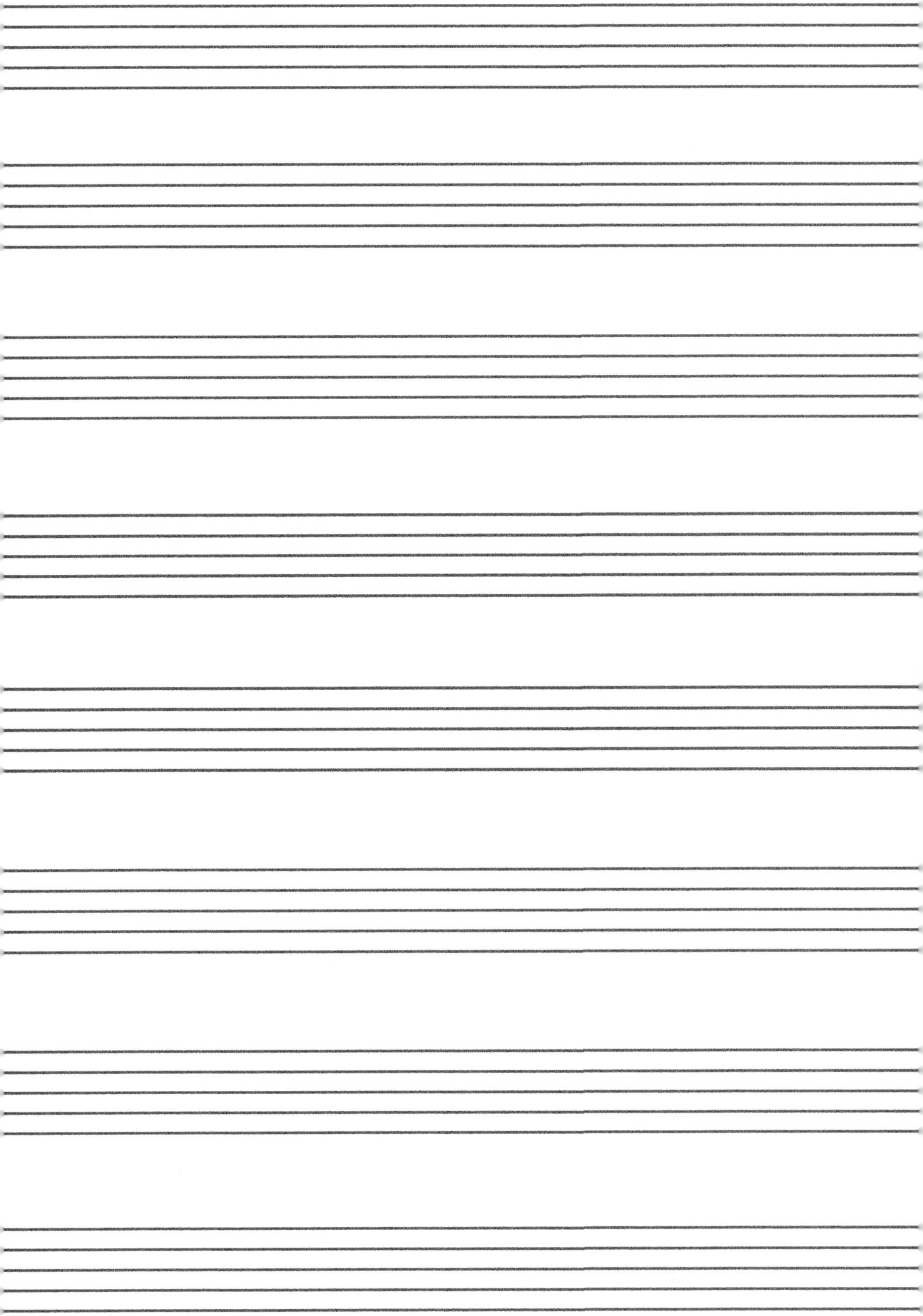

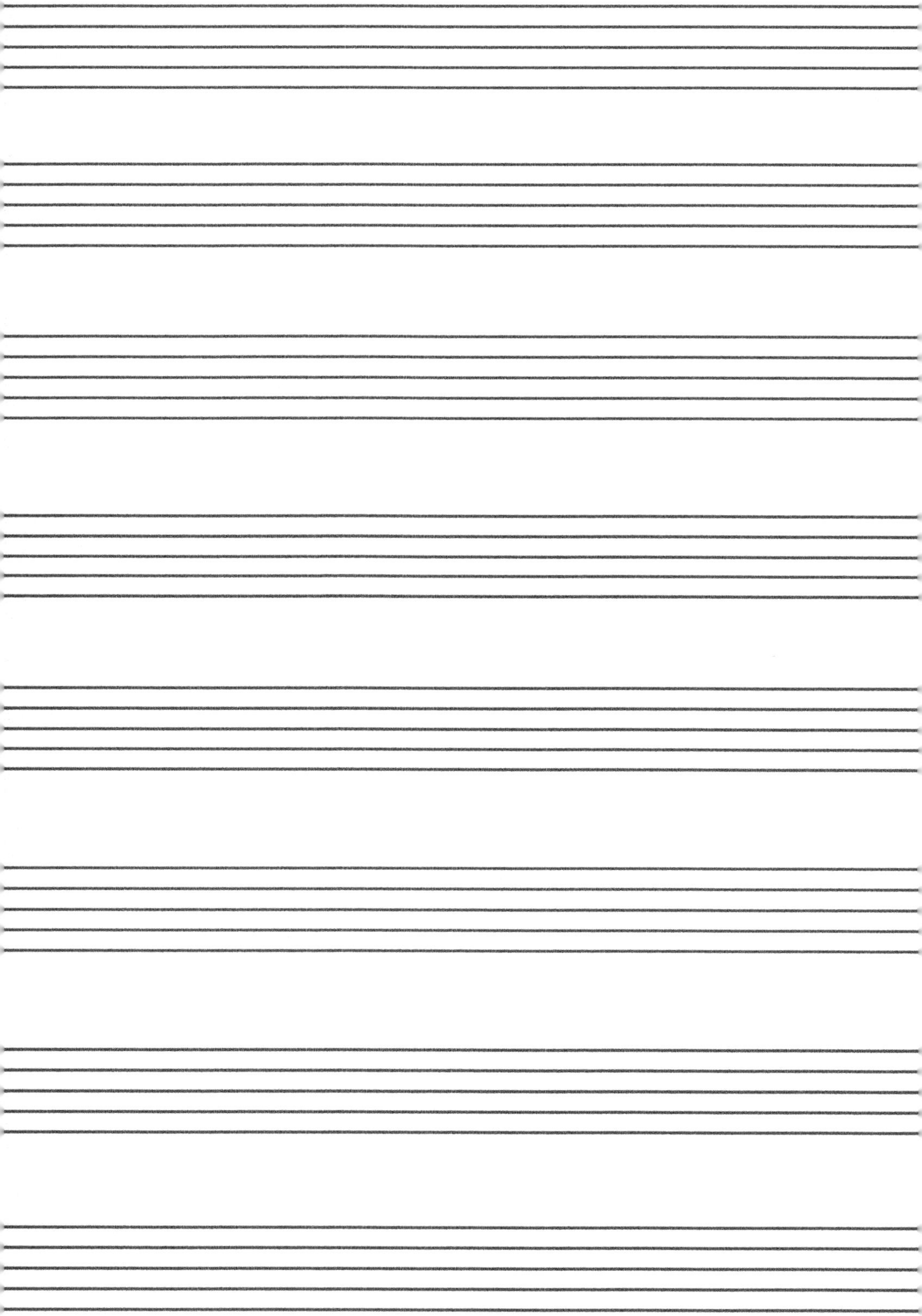

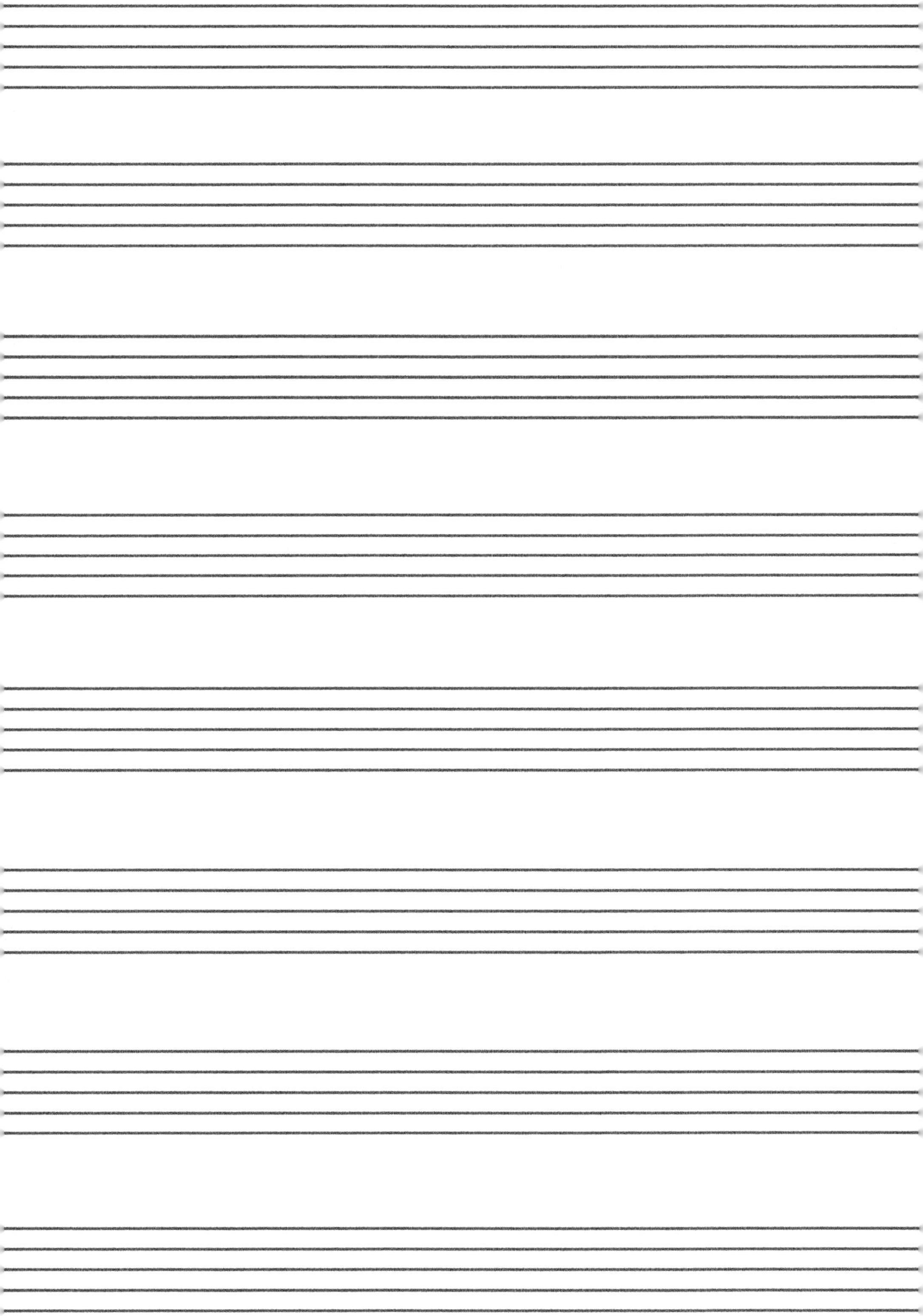

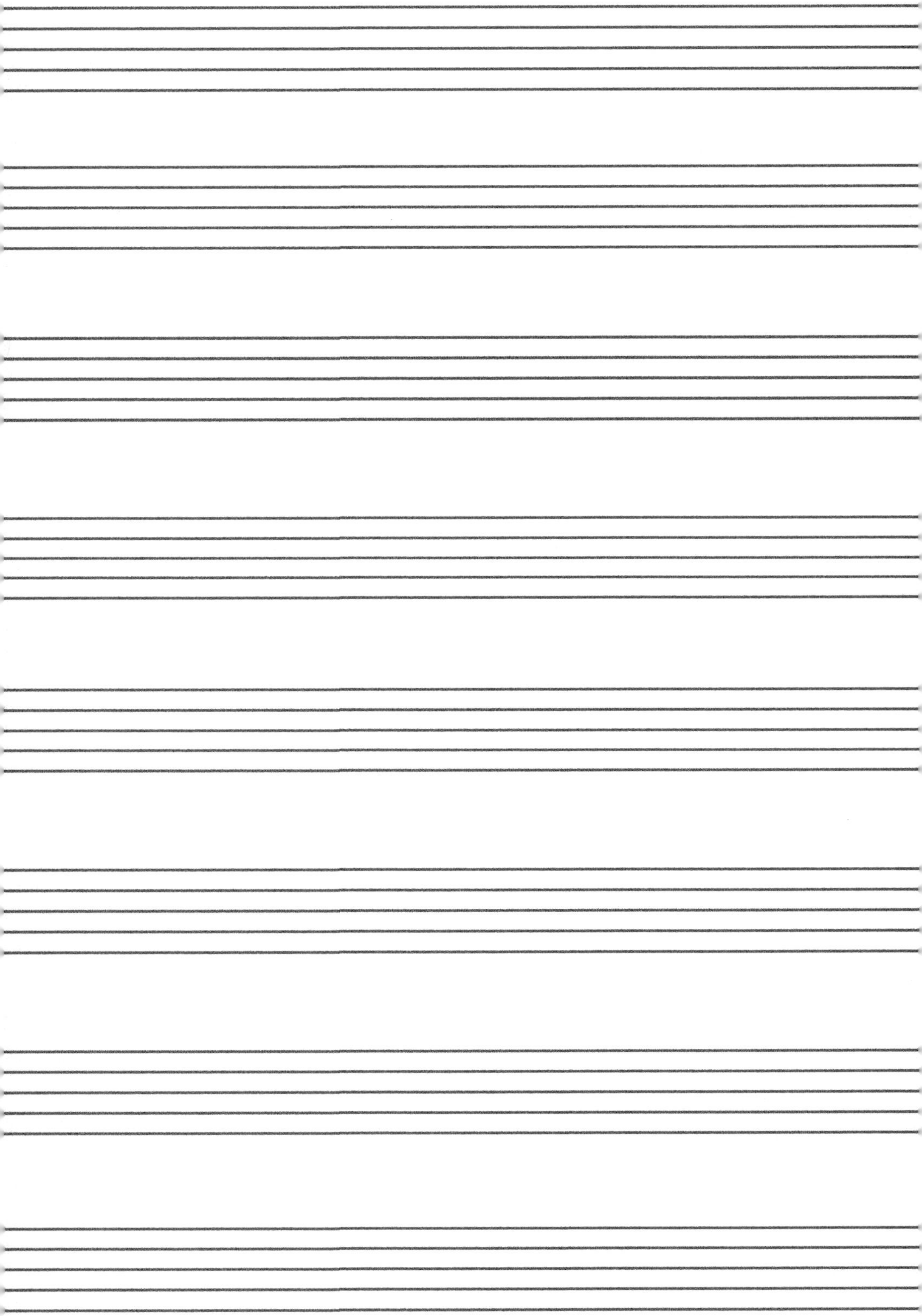

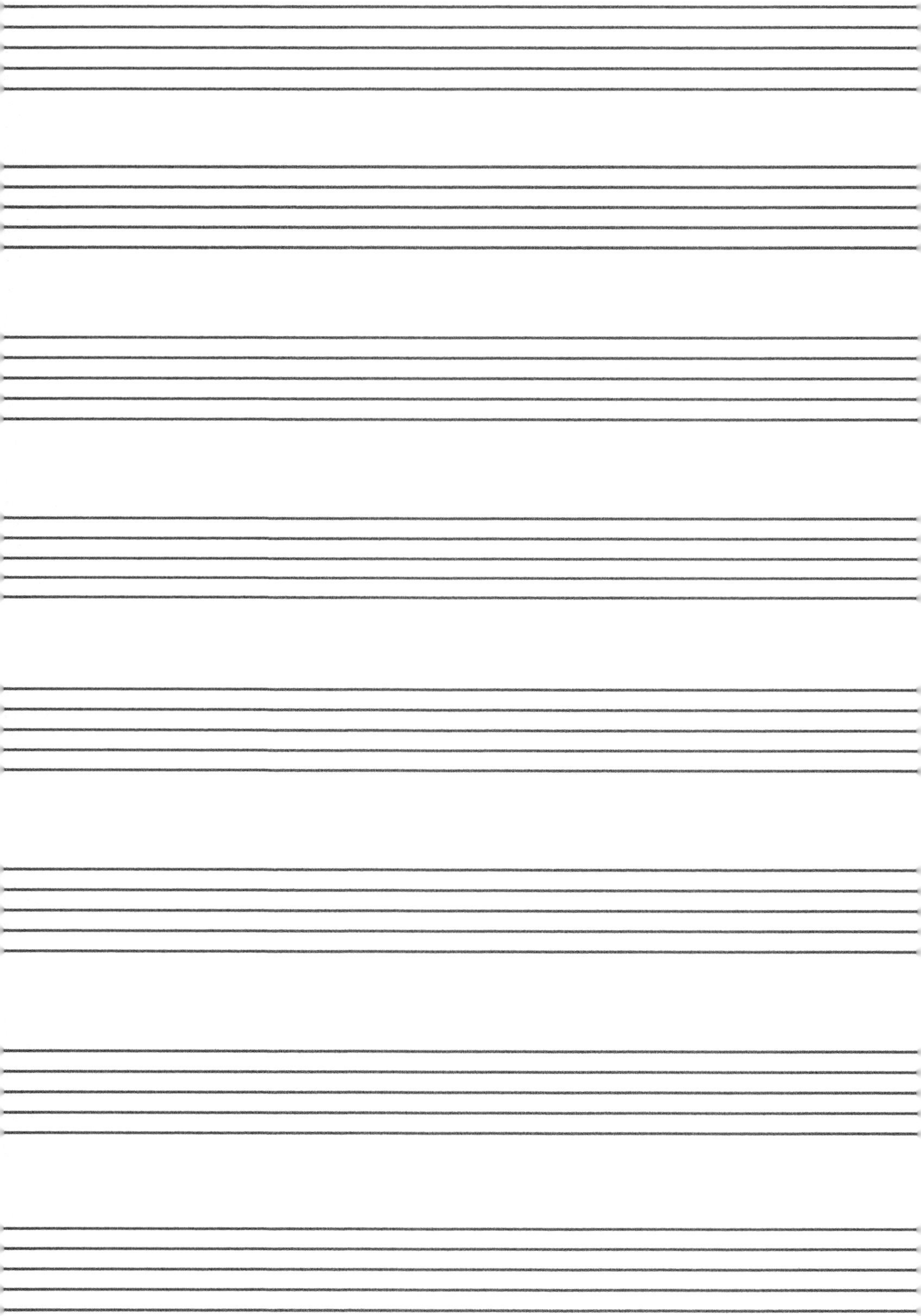

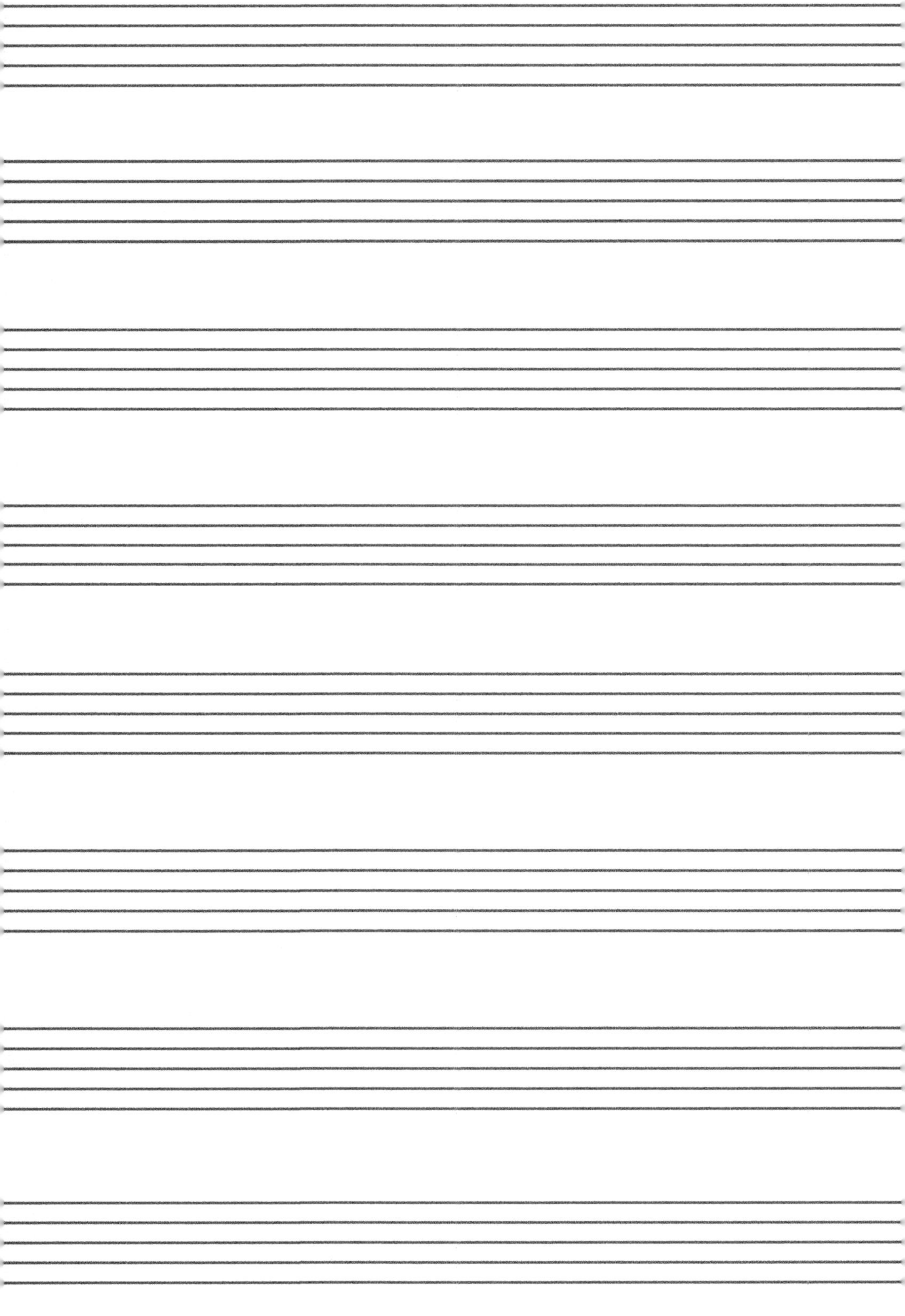

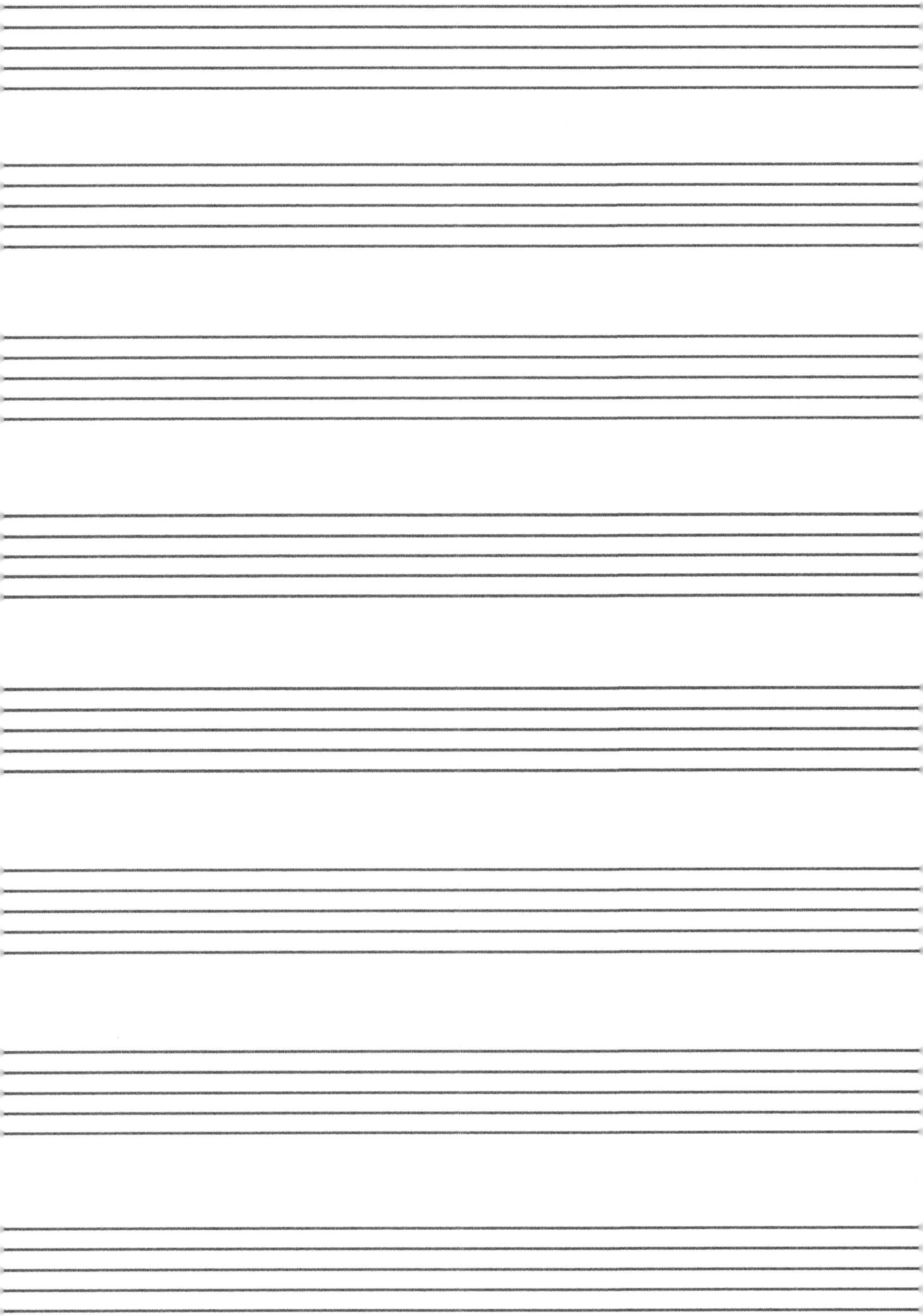

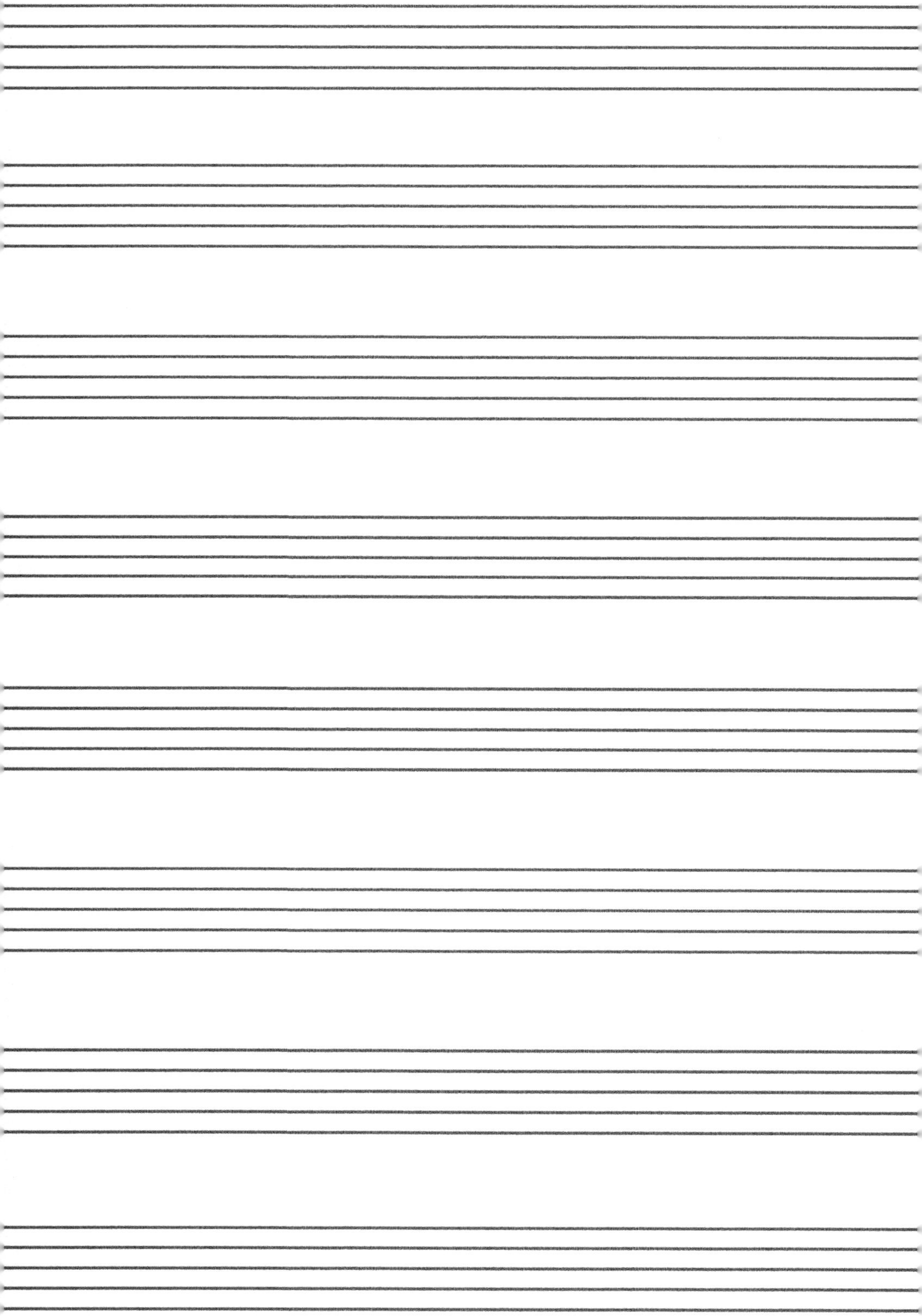

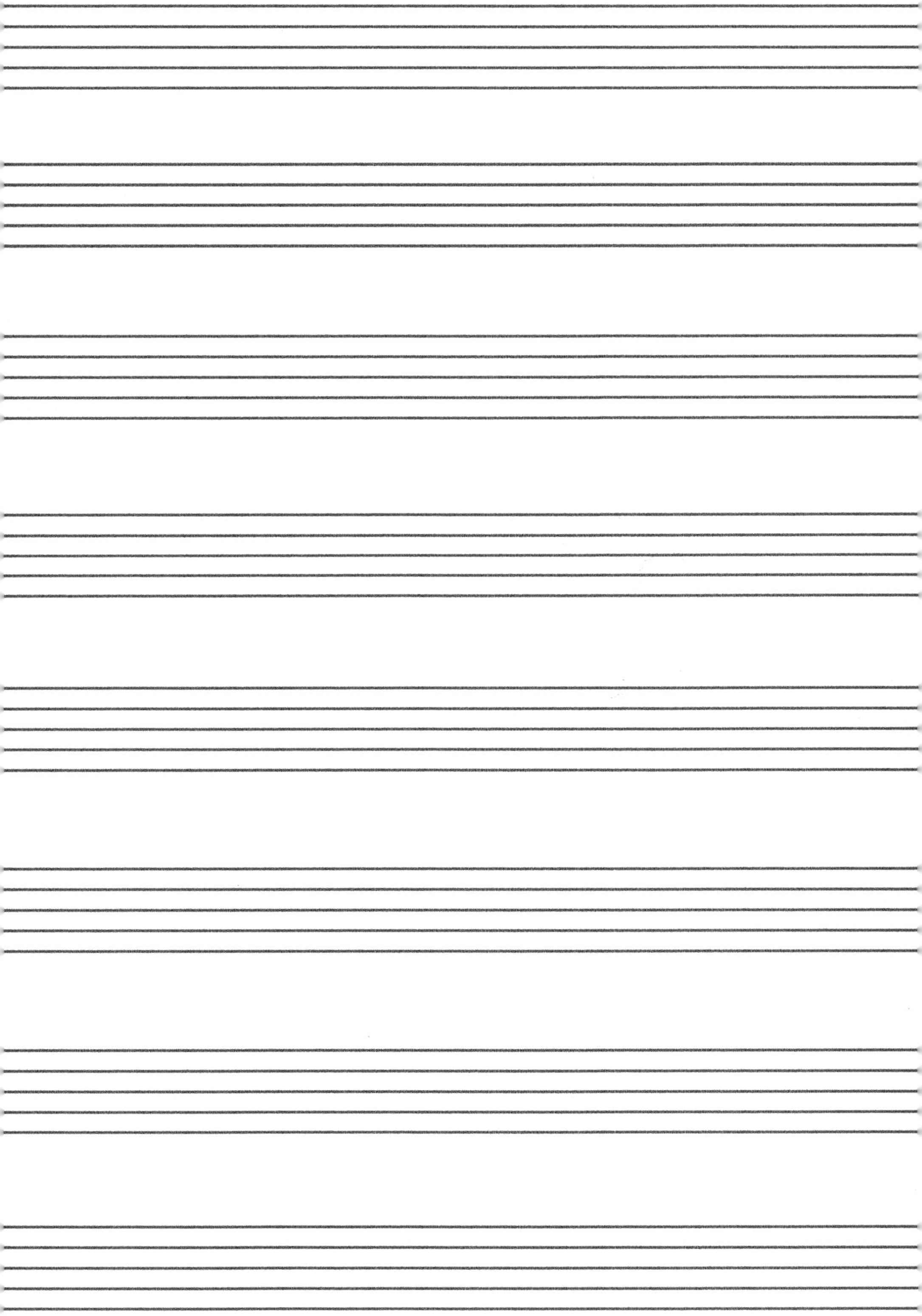

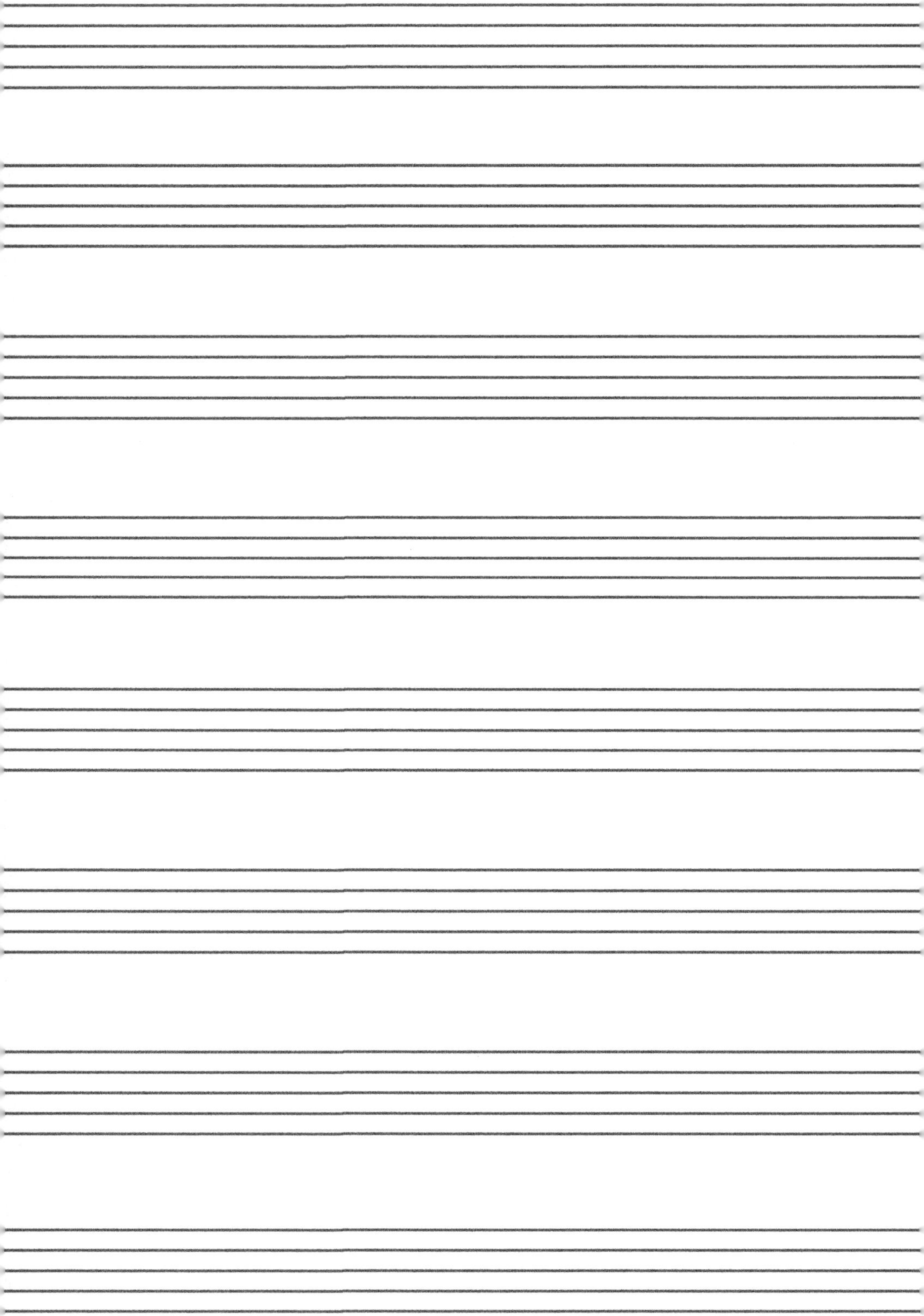

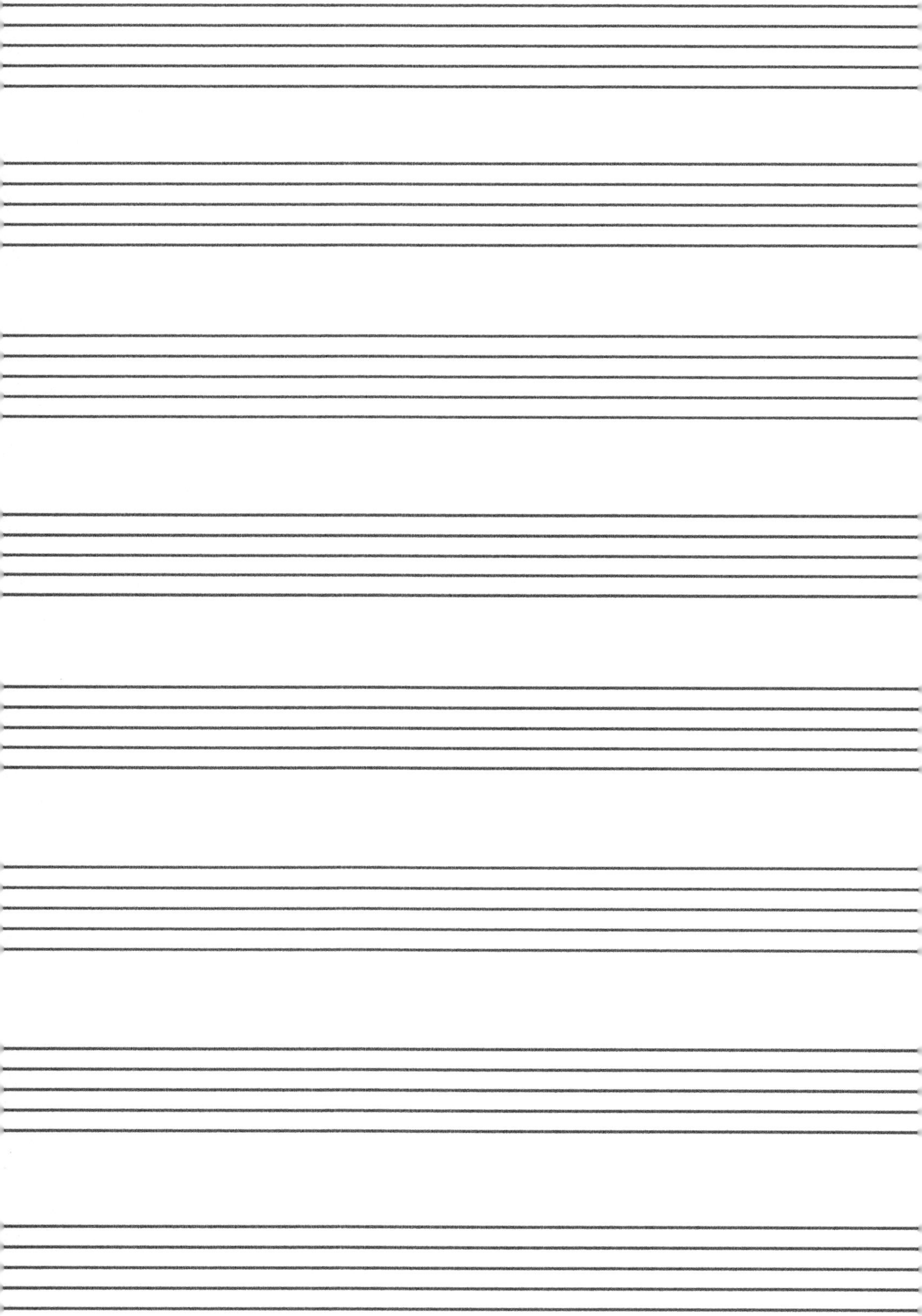

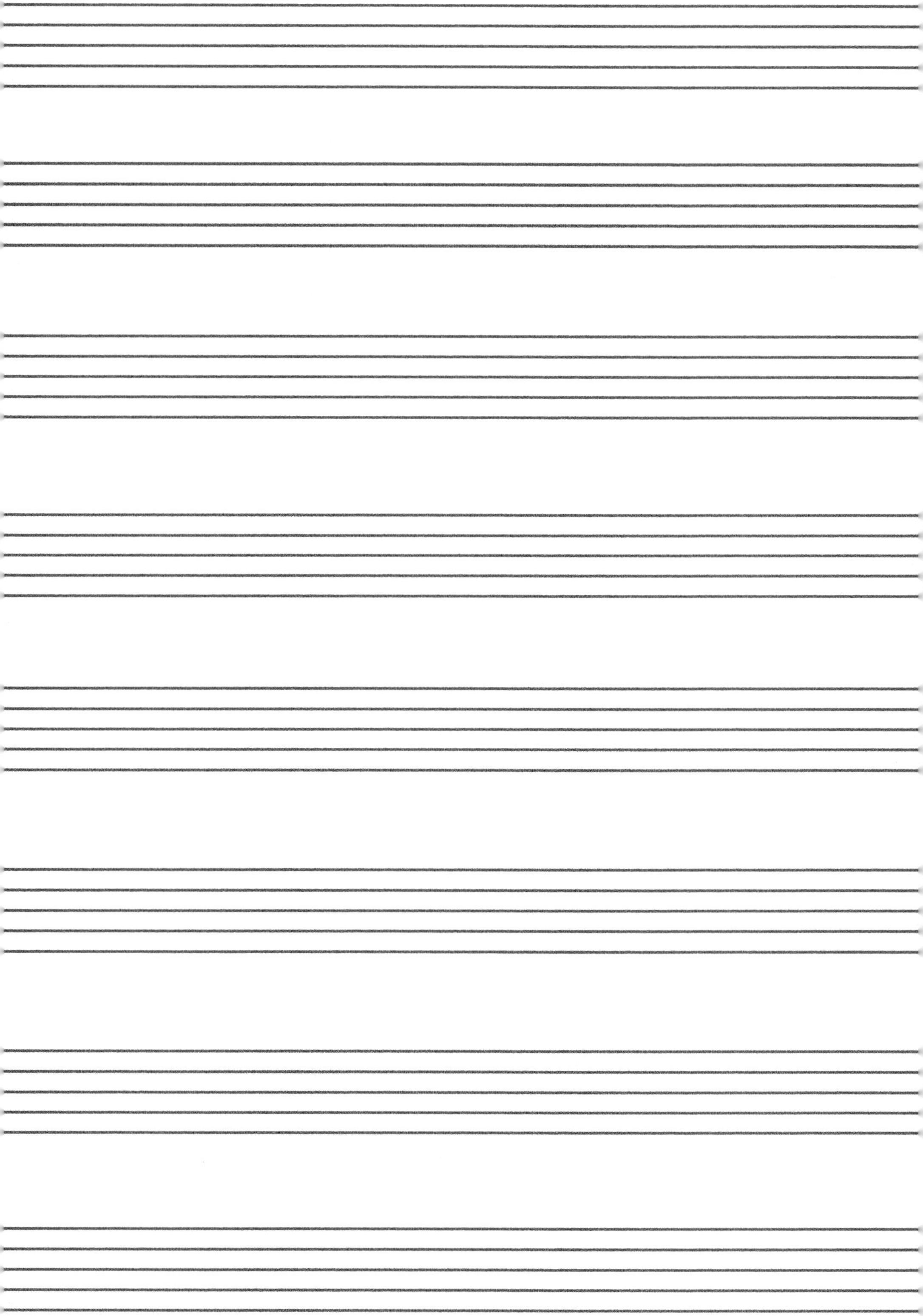

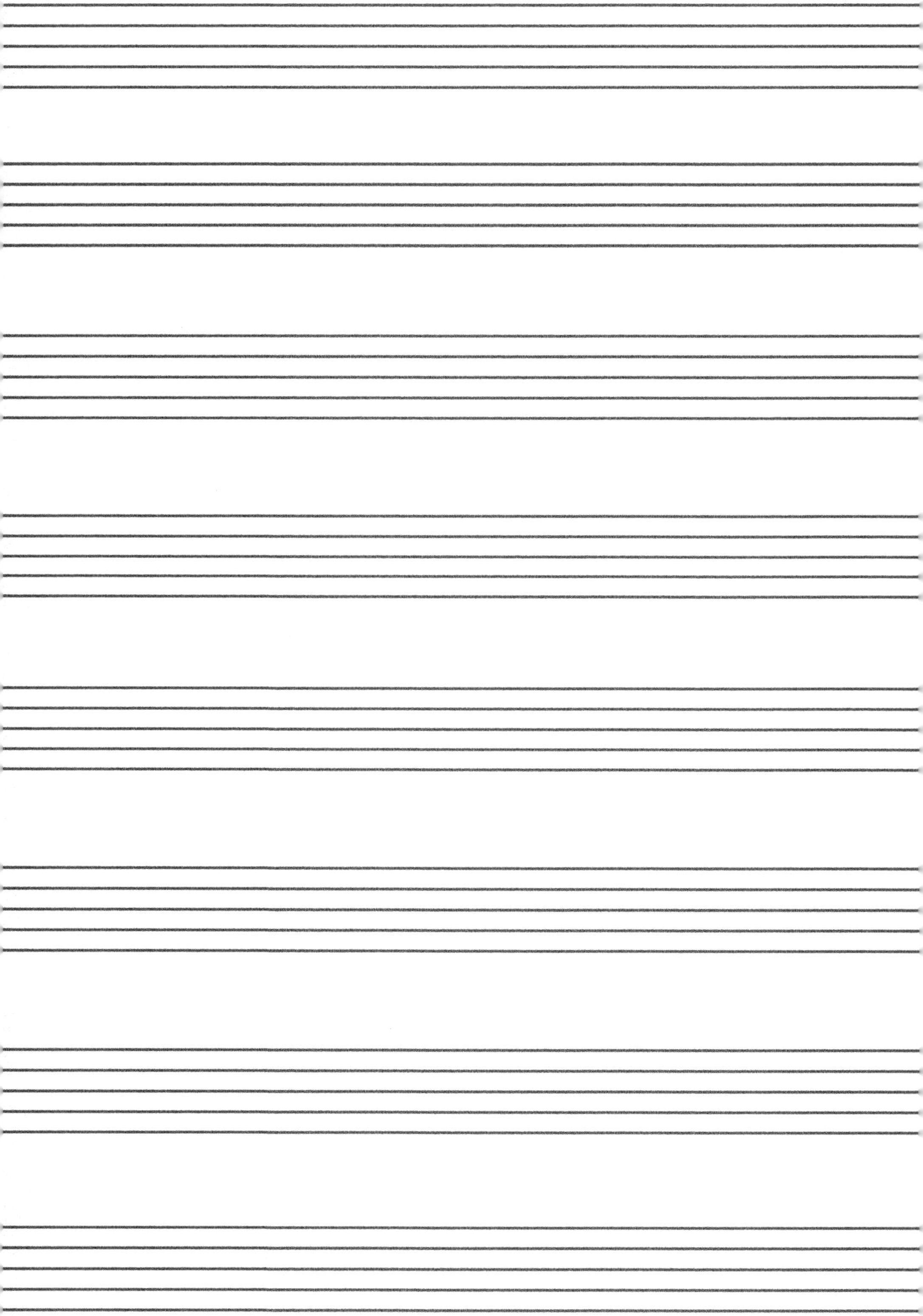

Made in the USA
Middletown, DE
09 September 2021

47916724R00070